LEOPOLDVILLE

BY JAKI MCCARRICK

Including the short story
The Congo

WWW.SAMUELFRENCH.CO.UK
WWW.SAMUELFRENCH.COM

Copyright © 2015 by Jaki McCarrick
All Rights Reserved

LEOPOLDVILLE is fully protected under the copyright laws of the British Commonwealth, including Canada, the United States of America, and all other countries of the Copyright Union. All rights, including professional and amateur stage productions, recitation, lecturing, public reading, motion picture, radio broadcasting, television and the rights of translation into foreign languages are strictly reserved.

ISBN 978-0-573-11099-3

www.samuelfrench.co.uk
www.samuelfrench.com

The Congo short story by Jaki McCarrick taken from *The Scattering* (Seren, 2013)

FOR AMATEUR PRODUCTION ENQUIRIES

UNITED KINGDOM AND WORLD EXCLUDING NORTH AMERICA
plays@SamuelFrench-London.co.uk
020 7255 4302/01

Each title is subject to availability from Samuel French,

depending upon country of performance.

CAUTION: Professional and amateur producers are hereby warned that LEOPOLDVILLE is subject to a licensing fee. Publication of this play does not imply availability for performance. Both amateurs and professionals considering a production are strongly advised to apply to the appropriate agent before starting rehearsals, advertising, or booking a theatre. A licensing fee must be paid whether the title is presented for charity or gain and whether or not admission is charged.

The professional rights in this play are controlled by Knight Hall Agency Ltd, Lower Ground Floor, 7 Mallow Street, London, EC1Y 8RQ

No one shall make any changes in this title for the purpose of production. No part of this book may be reproduced, stored in a retrieval system, or transmitted in any form, by any means, now known or yet to be invented, including mechanical, electronic, photocopying, recording, videotaping, or otherwise, without the prior written permission of the publisher. No one shall upload this title, or part of this title, to any social media websites.

The right of Jaki McCarrick to be identified as author of this work has been asserted in accordance with Section 77 of the Copyright, Designs and Patents Act 1988.

Author's Note

I wrote my short story *The Congo* before I wrote *Leopoldville*. I don't usually write plays based on my short stories but in this instance I did, simply because I could not get the characters from *The Congo* out of my head. Either I had not done with them – or they had not done with me. I remember seeing a middle-aged junkie in Dundalk (Ireland) in early 2008 and thinking he could be an older Terry Mansfield. Terry Mansfield is a fictional character (though his crime is based on a real-life crime) so obviously this is impossible. There was just something about the sadness in the man's eyes that reminded me of Terry, a character I had invented. So I knew then that I had yet to exorcise this gang of youths, and their story, from my imagination.

Around the same time, I read an essay by Edward Bond, his preface to *Saved* (Methuen), in which he correlates violent crime at home with war abroad (in the case of *Saved*, Vietnam) and police violence. I began to wonder why the real-life young men, upon whom *The Congo* is based, committed their crime, a matter explored more deeply in the play than in the short story. I came to the conclusion that geography and economics had everything to do with it: By 1990 Ireland had just suffered a decade-long recession to which there was no end in sight. Dundalk, an industrial town on the northeastern seaboard, was laid to waste and had unprecedented levels of youth unemployment. Described by the writers of the *Rough Guide to Ireland* (1989) as 'El Paso', this border town was also something of a buffer zone to the Troubles throughout the 1980s. So in many respects, *Leopoldville* is a political play, and in it I propose a socio-economic explanation for a very particular crime that occurred in a very particular part of Ireland.

I wrote the short story after some research; for *Leopoldville* I did much more, and pored over newspaper archives in my local library. The names of the boys who committed the crime were never published, and I guessed that two were brothers – which turned out to be the case.

In the short story I imagine Mansfield as an unreliable narrator who has returned to Dundalk to seek revenge on Devlin, who he believes has ruined his life. In the play, Mansfield is more innocent. So a few details shifted between story and play. And, as I was writing *Leopoldville*, I became aware that there was something ritualistic about the crime itself, and to develop this I turned to the pub's real name, 'The Congo', which of course was a gift in terms of expounding upon my theme of the roots of violence.

Many coincidences haunt both play and story. For instance, on the opening night of the play, in London, a member of the audience (who had, apparently, wandered in by chance) claimed to be the lawyer for the original boys who committed the crime. I was in Ireland at this time so did not get a chance to speak to him. In fact, I thought he might have been in attendance to check the play out for possible libel! Then, three years later, I read from my collection of short stories, *The Scattering* (Seren), at the 2013 Electric Picnic Festival in Stradbally. For some reason I chose to read *The Congo*. After I finished, a man came up to me and introduced himself. He was that very lawyer who had wandered into the play in London. His attendance at the reading was, he said, also accidental, as he had no idea what writers had been programmed to read that night. We discussed the crime. He said it was one of the worst cases of cruelty he'd ever seen and that after sentencing he gave up practicing law and became a craft brewer.

Also, at the first *Leopoldville* reading, at the Old Red Lion Theatre in London, in attendance were four people who had travelled over from Ireland to see the play. They were old friends of the real-life publican. They said I had somehow managed to capture the man's spirit – despite the fact that much of the story is fictional. They said that their friend would have most likely chatted and joked with the lads who had burgled his pub, as Prentice does in the play.

I wrote both works just before the most recent recession in Ireland, which began after the banking crash of September 2008. Seven years on there are towns all over the country still suffering from this recession and the devastating effects of austerity. If the story of *The Congo* and *Leopoldville* has a message at all it is this: the persistently depressed environment, particularly if it is also politicised, is a dangerous place for human beings; we simply don't do well without hope or prospects. In that respect the story is also something of a warning.

Jaki McCarrick
September 2015

Winner of the 2010 Papatango New Writing Prize, *Leopoldville* was produced by Papatango Theatre Company at the Tristan Bates Theatre, Covent Garden, London, on 7th April 2010. The cast was as follows:

JONAH DEVLIN .... Jack Ashton
PRENTICE BLACK .... Richard Hawley
GASCOIGNE .... Joe Sims
TERRY MANSFIELD .... Drew Webb
MIKEY CRILLY .... Russell Simpson
JOE CRILLY .... Chris Aylmer

Director .... George Turvey
Designer .... Helena O'Nions
Lighting .... Gary Bowman

> What huge imago made
> A psychopathic god:
> I and the public know
> What all schoolchildren learn,
> Those to whom evil is done
> Do evil in return.
>
> *'SEPTEMBER 1, 1939'*
> *W.H. Auden*

The Congo

A short story

When I awoke the first thing I did was check my bag. I took from it what I needed then tucked it back under the bed, placing my father's slippers neatly in front. I went to the window and opened it, amazed as I did that I remembered the bottom pane was loose. A grey cloud hung over the town, and three mallards the colour of barley flew in a line towards the Ramparts River. I wondered if I had been away at all, for everything was as it had been when I had left, twenty odd years before, except I could no longer hear the lowing of cows from Quincey's field, which was home now to a new housing estate. It had been like this since my arrival: encounters with my old self, a strange sensation of continuum, of picking up where I had left off. As if my London self was there still, walking through Richmond on his way to Kew, while my younger self, that ghost, was here in this damp house, staring out at the dawn weather.

I closed the door behind me, the smell of the eggs I'd fried for my father's breakfast still clinging to my nostrils, and walked to the corner of the tree-lined Avenue. The edges of my holster chafed at my ribs and sweat beads formed on my forehead making my face feel cold. I carried on down the Echo Road, past the freshly mown playing fields, on towards the Grange.

The place was as tranquil as I'd ever seen it. In the pale morning light even the houses with the smashed-in windows and weed-run gardens looked serene, so that the ragwort passed almost for daisies. There was a fabulous assortment of colours too, from the many flower baskets, filled as they were with petunias, begonias, violets. There had always been people in the Grange who would try to pull themselves up; always a mother or father prepared to stand up to the gangs.

From where I stood, I could see Devlin's place. The house seemed much the same: the satiny fuchsia hedge, the faux-Tudor windows gleaming like mirrors, the tall palm soaking up the rays of the early sun. Had he really returned, I wondered? Or had he gone, upon his release, to Kilburn, as some had said he had, where it was possible he'd been living under my nose all these months?

Grace had always been proud of her home. I'd always considered it a testament to her resourcefulness that when she'd found herself stuck in this estate on a widow's pension with six sons (two of them gang members), Grace had still managed to keep an attractive house. Fortress Devlin, she would call it, as she'd felt so safe within its walls. Built in the seventies, the Grange had promised the families that came to live in it – modernity: bathrooms, spacious bedrooms, central heating. But within a decade it had become a festering sprawl, filled with gangs, drugs, violence. And her husband's death before her boys were full grown ensured that Grace and her sons remained there, such is the quicksand nature of the ghetto, which requires money, time and strategy to get out of (and none of these had been much available to Grace). The air up on the Avenue had always been rarified and easy, while here, even now, I could feel the deadweight of Grange air in my lungs.

As I proceeded to the corner of the car park for the new Dunnes Stores (where once there had been a hill – 'the clump' – where gangs such as ours would meet for prearranged fights), I saw a figure walk towards the bottleneck opening of the estate. I moved in behind a van and, for a second, thought I might have been seen for the figure did not pass. A match was struck and tipped to the ground, a cigarette sucked upon. The man continued past the van and a row of wood-panelled houses, stopped at the end of the street by the tall palm, opened the gate. It was Devlin. And apart from the close-clipped hair and greying sideburns he'd hardly changed: the same casual self-assurance, the almost effeminate gait.

I became perturbed by something: my heart, pounding against my ribs. This was not how it was to have gone. Think of The Congo, I kept telling myself. Think of The fucking Congo. I closed my eyes, and for a few chilling moments supposed I was actually there.

*

"Where d'yez think you're goin', you lot?" Staunton leaned into the car and thumped the glove compartment open. He rummaged inside, probably looking for drugs or drink, and pulled out my book. *War and Peace*, he read out, venomously. Devlin stared straight ahead. None of us spoke. "Yez have been drinkin', am I right?"

"Aye. We're all under the affluence of incahol, Sergeant," Devlin replied, deadpan, at which the rest of us cracked up. Staunton bit his lip. Devlin reached out, grabbed the book, threw it back to me. At this I knew the cop would do one of two things. Either pull us over and quiz us, maybe roughly, with a slap to the back of Devlin's head, or he would leave it, sensing what so many others had: the stirring power of this young man with ink-black hair and obsidian-like eyes who spoke with alarming authority. Then Devlin drew close, whispered something inaudible into Staunton's ear. Something he had on him, something we could tell was sexual. The cop paled, was breathless, his appointed authority gone like a mirage, so much so that when he asked what had happened to the missing wing of my Hillman Hunter, I confidently responded that it had 'flown away'.

"Well, go on. To wherever you're off ta, but yez can't stop here," Staunton said, oblivious to the fact that we had just left the publican in a torrent of blood, his rooms upturned, his cash register emptied, his skull in pieces under a corn-yellow canister of gas.

We had not gone to bed that night. Under Devlin's orders, the twins had taken the simpleton, Gascoigne, into the cemetery and tied him with rope to a stone Celtic cross. Devlin had wanted to teach Gascoigne a lesson. To get him to keep his mouth shut about things he'd seen in his mother's B&B: somebody else's girl, somebody's wife. Mikey peeled the bananas while Joe forced them, one by one, into the lad's mouth. It was my job to watch over all of this. Watch, as the Crilly twins pissed on the poor wretch, bound and stuffed like a pig on a spit, the piss-steam rising off him like smoke. Under Devlin's orders we left Gascoigne in full-dark, wailing and crying for his mother. Then, later, when I'd slipped back to let the boy go, I saw Devlin walk him out of the cemetery, his arm around the boy. I imagined Devlin saying to Gascoigne that it was *he* who had saved him, that he would look out for him, like he'd done to me. That was how Devlin operated. Like all bullies, he sought out the feeble-minded, misfits and outsiders, who, having experienced the ferocity of his power also knew its narcotic warmth and radiance.

Later, after we'd left the bar and its publican for dead, I drove to the Cooley hills. All the way up the meandering lane, Adamski's *Killer* boomed (as if accusingly) from the car stereo. I parked the car by the gates. We clambered out and walked into the bog, sat high up on the plum-coloured heather.

I looked down at the town, all amber in the evening light, at the Irish Sea below us winding around the stark blue Mournes across the border. I felt cold. The hills filled with an icy sea-wind that closed around us like a cloak. I thought immediately of the Russian winter and the frostbitten Napoleonic soldiers of my book. And for the first time I doubted Devlin's leadership. Why had he let it go so far? The reality of the murder we'd just committed under his feverish spell suddenly hit me. I looked around. The twins had felt it too. They were both pale and slumped, huddled together on the mizzling day, like two spent sunflowers in October. Then Devlin walked up to us. I will never forget the way he did that. He churlishly took the twins' knives and twisted them into a bank of turf, hard and skinned-over since the council had prohibited cutting it a few years before. (The knives had not even been used that day.) Then he said he was *hungry*, that the cold mountain air had made him ravenous. I wanted to puke when he said that, and suddenly what we had done down there in the town began to seem as real and terrible a thing as Devlin's hunger.

I cannot remember exactly why he chose The Congo. I just remember that after the cemetery, Devlin said he wanted *to do some damage*. I had no idea he meant 'people damage'; I thought he meant burning something, or trashing some old house up, and I was ready, as ever, with my car.

"Where you thinking of goin'?" Mikey asked.

"Park Street," Devlin said.

"Class!" Joe said, and went on about being in for a day's drinking.

"No. No drink. That's not what I meant," said Devlin.

"What did you mean?" I asked.

"Well, somethin' will come. Somethin' will come and we will know." That was Devlin all over. So damned enigmatic. As if he had commune with someone other than his own present self. I would learn in court that this was a trait common to the likes of Charles Manson and Ian Brady, a means to avoid all guilt: *blame it on the voices, the signs, some force outside oneself.*

He was younger than me by two years, so by rights we should never have been friends. Only he saved me once. One night, up the alley by MJ's (where he and the twins drank), he'd stopped me from being kicked to death by a bunch of shit-kickers from Ardee. Only for that night I'd never have been part of the gang, or come to know him or the Crilly twins, or any of the lads from the Grange (after all, I went to the Grammar, and lived on the Avenue). I remember looking up, half-expecting the tall, dark-eyed interloper to join them, and, instead, he flung them off me like a wild cat. Then the twins charged in, dragged my two hick assailants towards the river. I never asked Devlin why he pulled me from that beating. I presume he saw in me what he later saw in Gascoigne: an exploitable weakness, such as the shame I wore like a badge as son of the town's most notorious drunk.

I sheltered in, and even came to like, the 'hard' reputation the Grange boys had. I hoped that by association it would rub off. Until my involvement with Devlin, I'd had to suffer all manner of quips about my family's change of fortune. From millionaires to hungry up in the big house (followed by the passing of my mother, who did what she did, some said, because she had felt so disgraced). So, by the time I fell in with Devlin, I was that fed up I no longer cared if people thought me a chip off the old block or not (and they definitely did). I began to justify their thoughts, became well and truly Mad Mansfield, the Drunken Solicitor's Son. I began to drink heavily, mindlessly sometimes; to gamble (anything – cards, horses, dogs, the slots*), so that I must have seemed like rich pickings indeed to Devlin with the amount of insecurities I had. Whatever way it happened, the way two people find their fate in one another, I was a troubled young man from the Avenue one day, and the next bewitched by a lout (albeit a beautiful lout).

Devlin called in to the bar. No one answered. The signs he'd been waiting for: no one around, middle of the day, cash register open.

For the first few minutes inside, the twins joked and pretended we were in the bar of a Western. The Congo was high-ceilinged, had never been updated. The wooden floors were dull and decorticated in places. The bar itself was breast-high with a gleaming brass rail hanging just beneath the rim of the bar top. Devlin sat on one of the red leather seats and lit up in his usual girlish way, slow and light, his little finger apart (erect almost), and watched the twins as they fooled around. I have never since met anyone, however duplicitous or skilled in the craft of acting, who could smile as sweetly as he – the smooth white baby-fangs, the gentle crescent dimples – yet possess a simultaneous deadness in the eyes. It was, I understand now, the overlapping of two people in one. He was night and day in one, and it was, for me, I recall, a hopelessly magnetic contrast.

"Mikey leave it!" Devlin said.

---

* = slot machines

"But Jesus man, the place is fuckin' empty!"

"You're tanked up enough. We might need to run for it. Use your head."

"Well, come on then!" Joe said. "We've got the money, what we waiting for? Let's go."

Devlin placed his long legs on top of the table, and crossed his feet. He put his arms behind his head, wrist to nape.

"Why would someone leave a place like this for scumbags like us to come and fuck around inside it, hah?" Devlin said.

"Maybe he's gone to get somethin'," Mikey replied.

"Who's he?" Devlin asked Mikey, who was now scared.

"Who's he?" Devlin repeated.

"Prentice Black he means," I said, 'the owner.' My father had known Prentice Black. People who came to the bar thought Prentice a survivor from an Irish UN battalion massacred in the Congo in the 1960s, and Prentice would let them think it. The truth was Prentice had bought the pub from a man named Cyril White in the same year the Congo had gone from being a Belgian colony to a Democratic Republic. Prentice (who had himself been a member of the 'old' IRA, i.e. pre-Bloody Sunday IRA), could not resist what he saw as a parallel between his purchase and the establishment of the African state, hence the pub's name (there was even a map of Africa in the shape of Patrice Lumumba's head in the men's toilets). When I suggested that Prentice might be over in the bookies opposite, it set something off in Devlin.

"Well, then we'll wait," Devlin said, coolly.

"Fuck's sake, why?" asked Joe. He and Mikey had become bored and restless in the dingy veneer-panelled lounge, the light a muddy olive colour from the stained-glass tiles above the windows. They had begun writing, with a black felt-tip marker, obscenities, on the wide mirror at the back of the bar.

"Hey, we'll wait, fuckwit, because a man that'd leave his bar in the middle of the day is a careless man. And in my experience, a careless man always has easy access to money."

It was then I started to become afraid. Mikey and Joe had between them taken over fifty pounds from the till. My pockets were stuffed with cigarettes, crisps, a bottle of Bombay Sapphire. We could have walked. That's what I wanted to do. Even the twins looked worried. For Devlin had implied something way beyond our usual messing. Even beyond the worst we, as a gang, had done up till then (which, apart from Gascoigne, had been the bottles we'd stolen for the Provos for petrol bombs). Yet we remained. Compelled as ever by that smile, by those black unforgiving eyes, by the magnetism I loved but had already begun to resent. And so minutes passed and we waited. I remember the silence. I remember wondering what he would do and how he might do it. I remember not knowing if I should run, or throw myself down and bathe in his glow. The room was like a theatre, all hush and darkness, as we, the actors (chorus and lead), waited in the wings for our audience to enter. And somehow I knew, through some inner sense, that when Prentice Black returned to his bar from wherever he had been, he would never leave.

Disturbed by a flapping sound, I quickly opened my eyes to find that I was a long way from those dark, unforgiving days of my youth: it was the leaves of the tall palm whipping at the air as if they would break loose. I watched the ravens caw over the rooftops of the Grange on their way to the Avenue's tall cedars where they nested. Again, I noticed it: the sensation of continuum. A trickle of smoke from the chimney of Devlin's house – though it was a warm morning, and I imagined Devlin in there looking after Grace.

I'd gotten seven years for my part in the murder of the publican. Devlin and the twins mandatory life. I'd blamed Devlin for all that had gone wrong with me since: my discovery of opiates, my involvement in importing scams.

I'd even learned how to use a gun; there are many such places in London. But standing here at the edge of the Grange, despite my anger, my hand would not reach into my holster, nor would my legs (as if in some kind of physical rebellion) carry me to his house. The dreams of retribution that had seen me through the years in London seemed suddenly impotent here. There was a sameness to the place that was obdurate, and I saw that my rage belonged entirely to the man who walked to his job at Kew each morning, whose only deliverance from this self and that, was time spent with the flowers and plants of the hothouses.

Of all the chilling details of that afternoon in The Congo bar, one image in particular stands out for me. Crossing the lounge to exit, I recall I'd looked across at the mirror, covered in the twins' spidery scrawls, and seen a skull-like face: eyes bloodshot from crying, blood on the hair and cheeks. I saw that the face belonged not to me, but to Devlin, who was looking in horror at something, or someone else, who or what, I could not fully see, for the light was poor. Perhaps, he looked at nothing in particular. Perhaps, he looked at me. I have often suspected as much. I remind myself on such occasions that though it was I, in the end, who had dropped the canister on the publican, neither Devlin nor the others had tried to stop me. In fact Devlin had screamed "down, Mansfield, down". His claims in court that he had meant for me to place the canister out of harm's way did not stand up under cross-examination (my own lawyer, a long-standing associate of my father, had emphasised my vulnerability, 'the fragility of one so young without a mother').

Finding solace in Devlin's greying hair, and in the fact he now lived an obviously uneventful life in the same wretched council house in which he had grown up, I walked back to the Avenue. But I felt bereft, too, knowing I would never again experience the intoxicating spell he had cast upon my youth. Grace had blamed 'the middle-class boy from the Avenue' and claimed that if anyone had been the protégé it was her son. But Grange people have always been (understandably) jealous of the affluent suburb that looks down upon them, and, I suppose, with all the harshness life had meted out to her, Grace is no exception.

CHARACTERS

JONAH DEVLIN – 18/19, unemployed son of a local Republican figure; cocksure, intelligent.

TERRY MANSFIELD – 19, student son of a local solicitor; intelligent, sensitive.

MIKEY CRILLY – 19, appears tougher than he is; has a job but wants to do better.

JOE CRILLY – 18, Mikey's brother. Joe is an unemployed barber.

GASCOIGNE – 21, has the mental age of ten; mother owns a local B&B.

PRENTICE BLACK, mid to late 50s, recently widowed publican. A man of vast experience.

A stroke (/) denotes the point of interruption in overlapping dialogue.

Set in 1990, in a border town, Ireland.

Note: If there is a health and safety issue in theatre concerning use of gas cylinders then barrels may be used instead.

Scene One

Cemetery. Old and overgrown. A summer's night, moonlit. A young, heavy-set man, **GASCOIGNE**, *is tied to an iron Celtic cross.* **MIKEY** *and* **JOE CRILLY** *are standing beside him, a box of bananas between them, skins scattered everywhere, a banana mess on* **GASCOIGNE**'s *clothes.* **JOE** *and* **MIKEY** *have just forced two half-peeled bananas into* **GASCOIGNE**'s *mouth. The skins drape over his chin.*

JOE Yah-hoo! That's it Gascy. Just. A couple. More.

> **JOE** *smashes both bananas into* **GASCOIGNE**'s *face.* **GASCOIGNE** *groans.*

> *Downstage,* **DEVLIN**, *smoking. He looks disapprovingly between* **JOE** *and* **MIKEY**, *then out at the surrounding fields.* **TERENCE MANSFIELD** *smoking downstage also. He is keeping watch, looking towards the road, while clandestinely drinking from a bottle of whiskey. Both are isolated in their own pools of light.*

Mikey. Bananas, please.

> **MIKEY** *throws a banana to* **JOE**. *They each peel a banana, force them into* **GASCOIGNE**'s *mouth.* **GASCOIGNE** *starts coughing.* **JOE** *puts his hand over* **GASCOIGNE**'s *mouth.*

Swallow.

MIKEY Do it.

JOE Ya hear me, bitch?

MIKEY Do it.

JOE Yah-hooh!

> **DEVLIN** *rushes over, takes* **JOE***'s hand off* **GASCOIGNE***'s mouth, pushes* **JOE** *against the wall of a vault.*

DEVLIN Said nothin' about chokin' him. Said nothin' about 'asphyxiation'. Know what that is dumbo?

> **MIKEY** *laughs.*

Shut up! Keep it simple 'n neat yez morons. One. At a fucken. Time.

> **DEVLIN** *lets him go, grabs a banana, goes up to* **GASCOIGNE**.

Now ladies. Watch. Peel. Hold the nose. Mouth opens. In ya go. Two inches. Close mouth. Wait. Right? That's better. Eh Gascy? That's it. You stupid fuckers.

JOE Yah-hooh!

MIKEY Dumbo!

> **JOE** *and* **MIKEY** *continue the force-feeding, one banana at a time.* **GASCOIGNE** *groans.*

> **DEVLIN** *takes the bottle off* **MANSFIELD**, *throws it aside.*

DEVLIN Some fucken sentry you are, eh? Drinkin' on the job. Shame on ya. Young buck like you. What's the world comin' ta, huh?

MANSFIELD Don't get it.

DEVLIN What?

MANSFIELD He's grand. Gascoigne. No trouble at all. He can't be much else as he's fucken retarded.

DEVLIN Not to do with you.

MANSFIELD I know his mother. She knew mine. She's all right.

DEVLIN She's a cunt.

MANSFIELD No, she…

DEVLIN She's a cunt and that's it. *(beat)* Unwritten rule in B and B, ya know? Unwritten rule about the biddy what owns it keepin' her pie-hole shut 'bout what she sees. Who she sees. Who she sees you with. Confidentiality it's called.

MANSFIELD That's Confession Dev. Not B and B.

DEVLIN Listen, our business is no one else's.

MANSFIELD He's retarded! He's hardly gonna be able to control his Ma and what she says, is he?

DEVLIN Well we'll see about that. *(long pause)* Ah, come on! Ya big… *(grabs **MANSFIELD** in a bear hug)*. Wanted to play, didn't ya? Wanted to play with the bad children, isn't that it?

MANSFIELD Yeah.

DEVLIN Then tough up fuck's sake. No one's dyin'. No one's gettin' killed. Right, Gascoigne? Right?

> **GASCOIGNE** *moans a response.*

Alive and well, see? Too fond a that piss you are. Brings ya down, that. Brings ya right down. *(raises voice)* People will talk, won't they Mikey.

MIKEY Talkin' already.

MANSFIELD Like what? What they saying?

JOE That you're a chip a the oul block. Just like him. Wino Mansfield.

> **MANSFIELD** *kicks at a stone, turns away.*

DEVLIN Oops. Hurt its feelin's boys.

MIKEY Joe, Jesus fuck!

MIKEY *jumps back.* **JOE** *is pissing on* **GASCOIGNE**.

JOE Eh-hey! What about this, Gascy, what about this! Cool ya down now, what? Wooh-hoo!

MANSFIELD You're disgusting. Lot a yez. Nothing but pigs.

DEVLIN Pigs is it? Now you want ta play – or pontificate? *(raises voice)* Or would ya rather me bend over and then ya pontificate?

MIKEY *and* **JOE** *make 'wooh' and 'sissy' sounds and whistles.*

MIKEY He might take you up on that offer, Dev.

JOE Aye. If ya drop an'ting make sure you kick it the whole way fucken home, Dev. (**MIKEY** *and* **JOE** *laugh*)

MANSFIELD Fuck off.

DEVLIN *(to* **MANSFIELD***)* Just keep your eyes on the road boy and your head straight and you'll thank me for it tomorra. *(to* **MIKEY** *and* **JOE***)* Come on pigs. Put that back in your trousers pig. Leave it now. That's it.

DEVLIN, **MIKEY** *and* **JOE** *walk off, lighting up cigarettes, laughing, screaming "wooh – hooh".* **GASCOIGNE** *is still tied to the cross, moaning and crying.*

MANSFIELD Shut up. *(beat)* Shut the fuck up, Gascy. You shouldn't have come, d'ya hear? Why'd you come?

GASCOIGNE *still crying.*

Oh, man. Come on, I'll get you home.

Undoes the rope and releases **GASCOIGNE** *from the cross.*

Here. *(gives* **GASCOIGNE** *a used tissue from his pocket)*

Clean yourself, fuck sake. Say nothing about this to your Ma, right? If it's not dry by time you get home tell her you fell in a puddle, all right? That's what you say.

GASCOIGNE *sobs. Sings a song to himself: 'He's the King of the Universe. J – E – S – U –S, yes! He's the King of me.'*

We're going home now, Gascy. That's it. Over.

Enter **DEVLIN** *with a coat. He wraps it around* **GASCOIGNE**, *softly wipes his hair and face.*

DEVLIN Now, now. Come on fella. *I'll* take ya home. See what Uncle Dev brought in his car for ya, huh? Better now, eh? What happened here… well, it will teach ya, yeah? (**GASCOIGNE** *nods*) What will it teach ya?

GASCOIGNE I don't know, Dev. I'll say nothin' about stuff I seen I 'spose. And my Ma. I'll tell her say nothin', like.

DEVLIN And what did ya see?

GASCOIGNE *(laughs)* Joe and some lady. You Dev, and you… *(beat)* Nothin'. I saw nothin'.

DEVLIN Aye. And what else does tonight teach ya, Gascy? Somethin' the same as not tellin' – only bigger.

GASCOIGNE Don't know Dev, don't know.

DEVLIN It'll teach ya not ta *betray* us. Which is the point of everythin' here this night, ya see? Especially not to your fucken cunt Ma. Who is a biddy bitch. It'll teach ya not ta take the piss outta the bad children.

GASCOIGNE I won't do that no more. I won't do that no more. You betcha.

DEVLIN Good. And who is your friend now and forever and ever?

GASCOIGNE You are Dev, you are.

DEVLIN And what will I do for ya from now on, Gascy?

Beat. **GASCOIGNE** *thinks.*

GASCOIGNE You'll watch over me.

DEVLIN That's it. Just like a...

Beat. **GASCOIGNE** *thinks.*

... somethin' with wings.

GASCOIGNE Is it an angel Dev, is it?

DEVLIN That's it my friend. *(he kisses him on the cheek and looks at* **MANSFIELD***)* Just like an angel.

> **DEVLIN** *goes to the edge of space with* **GASCOIGNE**, *points him off towards the car,* **GASCOIGNE** *exits.* **MANSFIELD** *looks for, and finds, his bottle. Drinks remains.* **DEVLIN** *stands in the darkness, watches for a few seconds.*

You'll not find her at the bottom a that.

MANSFIELD What you know about it?

DEVLIN Should be gettin' used to the idea by now, I'd say. Gettin' *over* it like. Been a year at least I reckon.

MANSFIELD I don't be thinkin' of her at all.

DEVLIN Good. Because if she was anywhere she'd be up there, wouldn't ya say? *(points to the sky)* Lookin' down on this shitehole town. Nose up, lookin' down on us all.

MANSFIELD I'll catch up with yez later.

Beat.

DEVLIN What ya lookin' at?

MANSFIELD Ah. The houses down there. With the lights. The people – all tucked up, happy and warm.

DEVLIN Ya know nothing about lives of those people. Grass-is-greener-itis you have, that's what. You're outside. Inside always looks good from there.

MANSFIELD *laughs at this, turns to* **DEVLIN**. *They catch each other smiling.*

That's it. Start – enjoyin' yourself. Have. A. Laugh. No one will think less of ya, Terry. We – I – won't think less a ya. That's all I'm sayin'.

MANSFIELD Yeah.

DEVLIN Well then, lets go.

Beat.

MANSFIELD Did ya – did ya ever watch the little moths that flit around streetlamps, Dev?

DEVLIN No.

MANSFIELD Just that – sometimes I think I'd be like one of those moths. Wherever the light is – I follow. Like I'm compelled, or hypnotized, or somethin'.

Beat.

DEVLIN Yer as queer as fuck, Terry Mansfield, that's what. The way you talk sometimes.

MANSFIELD Well, ya know what they say, Dev… *(he turns round and looks at* **DEV***. The look is held for a few seconds)*

DEVLIN *(stern)* C'mon now. Gascy's waiting.

MANSFIELD *turns around and exits,* **DEVLIN** *waits, looks at him, then out at the fields, at the houses with the lights. Exits.*

Fade lights.

Scene Two

Next day. Inside of a bar. Through the window the outside sign can be seen: 'The Congo' is written in large black letters. The background image on the sign is of mountains – with an image of a drum, fore-grounded. The sign swings in the breeze for a few seconds, an audible squeak. Inside: a breast-high bar with a brass rail; a silver faux-antique cash register; assortment of drinks at the back; red leather seats, red-velvet-topped bar-stools, a faded wooden floor; a number of black and white photos of a man in exotic places, getting off planes and ships etc, lining the walls. In some pictures the man is depicted with African tribesmen. On one wall there are two small drums, hanging high up. Downstage right, on the wall, where the bar ends, is a dartboard and blackboard – with a little ledge, which holds pieces of chalk and a case of darts. A face – **MIKEY**'s *– peers through the window, joined by* **JOE**. *They both disappear – then the door is opened slowly by* **DEVLIN**. *The bell of the bar rings out.*

DEVLIN *stands in the doorway, alone. The light picks out no detail of his face or figure, so that his momentary stance in the doorway is shadowy and ominous.*

DEVLIN Hello? *(beat)* Hey! Hello?

DEVLIN *indicates to others.* **MIKEY** *and* **JOE** *enter – with* **MANSFIELD** *last.* **MANSFIELD** *checks that no one has seen them enter the pub, then closes the door behind him.*

JOE Hell-o?

MIKEY *and* **JOE** *go to door leading upstairs, shout up* 'Hello? Hello?'

MIKEY Place is fucken empty.

JOE Wah-hoo!

DEVLIN Pull the curtains.

> **MANSFIELD** *walks over and pulls the half-curtains.* **JOE** *and* **MIKEY** *go to the bar and start messing around, jumping on the bar, getting excited, doing gun-slinging moves as if in the saloon of a Western, banging the bartop like a drum, grabbing at the crisps.* **JOE** *stands on the edge of the leather seats, starts tapping the small drums that hang from the wall. Bangs out the drum intro to Joy Division's 'Atrocity Exhibition'. Sings the words of that song: 'This is the way, step inside. This is the way, step inside'. Then jumps onto the floor.*

JOE *(acting)* Stop yer hemmin' and hawin' and draw why don't ya?

MIKEY *(acting)* Pow! Pow! Pow!

> **JOE** *screams and falls over the bar.*

Stop yer squallin' little fellar.

JOE *(as himself)* Don't call me that. I'm bigger than you, Mikey. By a long shot.

MIKEY *(as himself)* Ah fuck you. No good playin' cowboys with you when you can never just die. Just like Ma says. You can't keep still for shit.

DEVLIN Hey Mikey, check upstairs will ya? Joe, go with him.

> *The two grab a couple of beers from behind the bar. They snap the caps off; guzzle on beer, exiting stage right, towards 'upstairs'.* **DEVLIN** *sits down on one of the seats, places his feet on the table. Looks at* **MANSFIELD**.

Stinks in here. *(pause)* Said it stinks in here. Don't you think it stinks?

MANSFIELD His wife died. Maybe she was the one kept it clean or something.

DEVLIN Could do with a polish. Some flowers, maybe. Wouldn't ya say?

MANSFIELD Dunno. I don't drink in here. Nor my da. Far as I know.

DEVLIN Your da doesn't come here.

MANSFIELD That's it.

DEVLIN Doesn't drink in here.

MANSFIELD That's it.

DEVLIN Drinks in Vinegar Man's.

MANSFIELD Sometimes.

DEVLIN With the wife-beaters and alcoholics.

MANSFIELD Leave it alone will ya?

DEVLIN Alls I meant was it's a bit smelly, that's all. Mr. Black's not been lookin' after his pub.

MANSFIELD Only afternoon, Dev. Plenty of time ta be cleaning it.

Sounds of the other two stamping around the room upstairs.

DEVLIN Never been in here before. Well, we missed nothin'. It's a right oul kip.

MANSFIELD Shop-owners round this way – they come in. Chamber of Commerce heads. He's travelled round, Mr. Black has. Tells people about it. Talks all the time about his travels.

DEVLIN Who gives a fuck about it? Listen to music I say. Some Acid House. The Mondays. That's what ya want.

MANSFIELD Anyway, he's not upstairs. Ya can call them two off for a start.

DEVLIN Where's he then? *(*MANSFIELD *sighs and goes towards door.)* Where ya think yer going?

MANSFIELD Fucking home! I need to go. We all do. This is daft. Come on, my head's wrecked.

DEVLIN What I say before we came in?

MANSFIELD You said 'go hard or go home'.

DEVLIN After that.

MANSFIELD One more adventure.

DEVLIN One more adventure and that's it. We'll call it a night then.

MANSFIELD It's the next fucken day, Dev!

DEVLIN So it is.

MANSFIELD What can we do here anyway, tell me? What? Booze? I've any amount of it. Don't need to put ourselves at risk for booze.

DEVLIN Who said anythin' about booze? I know I didn't.

JOE and *MIKEY can be heard screaming and roaring as they fool around in the living-quarters area of the pub.*
MANSFIELD goes to the stairs. Calls:

MANSFIELD Come on down the fuck you two! We're leaving.

DEVLIN goes to MANSFIELD, pulls a knife and viciously points it at his throat.

DEVLIN Don't you ever call a shot like that in front of me, ya hear fucker?

MANSFIELD Yeah.

Beat.

DEVLIN You shouldn't make me do that to ya. Why'd you do that?

MANSFIELD I don't know.

DEVLIN S'pose you can't help it. Your Ma and all. *(pause)* Ya know, I was thinkin' a callin' ya what they called ya in school, yeah? Before they kicked you out, like.

MANSFIELD Yeah?

DEVLIN Tolstoy. Wasn't that it?

MANSFIELD Aye. Yeah.

DEVLIN War and fucken Peace. You read that book when you were how old?

MANSFIELD Twelve.

DEVLIN You clever fucking bastard.

MANSFIELD I liked reading. My Ma –

DEVLIN She's dead, Tolstoy.

MANSFIELD She wasn't that time.

DEVLIN No. *(pause)* You said he's not here. What d'ya mean by that?

MANSFIELD Nothin'.

DEVLIN Nothin'? Well get this, Terry. Terry Tolstoy who is supposed to be so fucken smart. Any man that'd leave his pub open and empty in the middle of the day is pretty fucken careless, wouldn't ya say? I mean it stinks. He hasn't cleaned it right. Everything's done halfways kind've. Yet he went out. Out without closin'. Look, I bet he *(interrupts himself, rushes over to the till, presses several keys, it bounces open, holds up a few notes)* … ya see Terry, what I'm tryin' to get across ta ya is – a man that'd leave his pub open, his curtains open, his <u>cash</u> <u>register</u> <u>unlocked</u> – for the likes of us scumbags to come in and fuck around inside is obviously a careless type of a man. And a careless type of a man, I'd say, would have easy access to money.

Beat.

MANSFIELD Say that again. A careless type of a man...

DEVLIN ... would have easy access to money. Money lyin' around. Money hidden. Money someplace.

MANSFIELD How do you know? I mean... /Jesus.

DEVLIN *(rapidly)* Look, he owns a pub so the man has money. He didn't lock it so the man is careless. Clear enough, no? So my feelin' is, the chances of somethin' like a stash of money lyin' somewhere, hidden somewhere... and not this piddlin' shit, a few quid... are pretty high, wouldn't you say?

Pause.

MANSFIELD Let's take the till money and go. Come on.

DEVLIN What I say two minutes ago?

MANSFIELD You said don't call the shots.

DEVLIN And what ya doin'?

Silence. **MANSFIELD** *shuffles around awkwardly.*

Yeah. And you're tryin' my patience doin' it. And I don't like ta hurt ya, Terry. Ya know that.

Pause.

MANSFIELD So maybe he's careless. His wife died. Maybe he's griefstricken. And maybe he has money lying somewhere. So what! A few bob. We should still just walk. In my humble fucking opinion Dev, that's what we should do. (**DEVLIN** *says nothing. Pours himself a coke, adds ice)* You don't care do ya? Well you're goin' a long ways on a *feelin'* Dev. That's all I'll say.

DEVLIN Confident of my understandin' of people and how they tick, Terry, that's all. Call it an instinct, if ya like. Now. Where would a careless man hide his secret stash of cash, I wonder? What would ya say about that, Terry?

MIKEY *and* **JOE** *enter laughing and drinking.* **MIKEY** *spews a line of beer between his teeth.*

Put the fucken booze down. *(they do)* What I say about booze?

MIKEY Not yet, ya said.

DEVLIN That's it. Ya want ta be found drunk on the floor by the cops, do yez? Caught red-handed like the stupid fucken cunts yez are? What's the story?

MIKEY No one up there boss.

JOE No one and no thing.

DEVLIN What d'ya mean 'no thing'?

JOE He has fuck all things.

MIKEY No telly, no music.

JOE No dirty magazines.

MIKEY Nothin'. Just an oul bed, whole load of books, fucken ornaments, maps, crappy radio, weird shit, fucken pictures, some kinda fucken spear, fucken lion skin…

JOE Leopard…

MIKEY Some fucken animal anyway. Travel shit. Shit ya see on wildlife programmes. Nothin' worth anythin' at all.

JOE Nice day out there, Dev, ya know? We should get outta this stink-hole.

MIKEY Give it a rest, Joey.

JOE *(to* **MIKEY***)* Well, isn't that what you said on the stairs? 'I think we should get out of this stink-hole.' Isn't that what you said?

MIKEY I said it to you.

DEVLIN We're goin' nowhere lads.

Pause.

MIKEY Fuck all here, Dev. That's the truth.

DEVLIN Tell them the conclusion we came ta about Prentice Black. Go on Terry. Tell them the conclusion.

Beat.

MANSFIELD Well… he… we… reckon… a careless man… the like of Prentice Black… must have… would have… could have… easy access to money. More than what's in the till, anyway.

JOE What the fuck does that mean?

MANSFIELD Means it's – here. Maybe. Somewhere. Money. Somethin'. Probably. But –

DEVLIN No buts or I'll gut ya, Tolstoy, I promise ya that…

MANSFIELD … but maybe we won't have ta go to the bother of looking… was what I was going to say. Because I, because I know where he is.

MIKEY Where then? Where is he?

JOE Yeah! You some sort of, whadyamacall, sidekick?

DEVLIN Psychic! Ya moron!

MANSFIELD Look: I seen him often enough. Sitting across the road in Tote. Talking about back-in-the-day and all his travels. Likes to do big bets, yankees. Knows about form and such. Gets all quiet when he loses. Big racing day today, see. And the main races are over in a couple of hours. In about two hours. So I say he'll be back. I say he'll be back in not much more than that.

Blackout.

Scene Three

>**MIKEY** and **JOE** playing Darts.

MIKEY Bulls fucken eye!

JOE Fuck ya. Give it here.

>**JOE** grabs the dart off **MIKEY** and fires it at his foot. **MIKEY** screams. **MANSFIELD** and **DEVLIN** laugh. The dart has penetrated **MIKEY**'s shoe.

Wooh-hoo! Double fifteen to me y'oul pig.

MIKEY You bastard. Get it outta me.

JOE Going nowhere now, are ya? Not the big darts player now, are ya? Not the big anythin'.

DEVLIN Take it out, Joe.

JOE Can take it out himself, big show-off.

DEVLIN Take it out!

>Pause.

>**JOE** walks over and takes the dart out. **MIKEY** screams. **MIKEY** pushes **JOE**, who is knocked back and starts to cry.

JOE You're fucken for it. Wait till Da gets ya. Your lights'll be knocked out. He'll fucken kill ya, he will.

DEVLIN (walks up to **JOE**, picks him off the ground an inch or two) Not if you keep your mouth shut he won't. Ya big girl's blouse ya! (the others laugh. Throws **JOE** down) Two Cokes. Plenty of ice. Two packets of crisps please, Joe.

>**JOE** gets up.

JOE Yez are always pickin' on me. Fucken sick of it.

JOE *goes over to the bar, gets the Coke-on-tap, flings it into two pint glasses, puts ice in. Stops.*

Two cokes. What flavour crisps?

DEVLIN What d'you reckon, Terry? You a cheese and onion – or a salt and vinegar man? What d'you say, Mikey? *(who is moaning in a corner)* What d'you say Mikey, 'bout Terry's crisps?

MIKEY Salt and vinegar.

DEVLIN Joe?

JOE What the fuck do I care?

DEVLIN Because you need to know what crisps to bring us, useless prick. We're customers.

JOE Well, on pain of death I'd say he was salt and vinegar.

DEVLIN As would I.

MIKEY After all, vinegar's in his blood.

DEVLIN Like Jesus. *(they laugh)*

MANSFIELD Jesus didn't have vinegar in his blood. He was just given it on a sponge – by a centurion.

Beat.

DEVLIN But that's what I meant, Tolstoy. That's what I meant.

MIKEY Would ya listen to it. I hate fucken students.

JOE *rolls down his sleeves over his wrists, throws his hair over his eyes, sucks in his cheeks, becomes slumped.*

JOE Man, I'm so superior. I'm so depressed. Give me fucken money. Who gives a shite about ya?

DEVLIN Cokes Joe please!

MIKEY Ya hurt my foot, Joe. Feels infected. (**JOE** *brings over the cokes and crisps*)

JOE Good enough for ya. Hope ya die.

MIKEY Say that again to me and I'll flitter ya with this dart.

DEVLIN We need to just sit here, civilised as is humanly possible with you two amadawns, and wait. For one man. Yez think we can manage a wee thing like that? Do ya, Joe? Mikey? And stop fucken tryin' to get under poor Tolstoy's skin here. He can't fucken help it if his father's a fucken scabby drunk. Worst in town. Gambled away the big hotel, and what was it, Terence? Oh yeah – big house up there on the Crescent. He can't help his father done all a that.

JOE Nor what happened to the poor mother.

MANSFIELD Say one more word about it and I'll…

DEVLIN And you'll fucken what?

Pause.

MANSFIELD I'll leave.

MIKEY AND JOE Wooh…

DEVLIN Will ya? Will ya fucken leave? Jesus, he'll leave, boys. Jesus, that's a fucken terror. What is that boys?

MIKEY AND JOE A holy fucken terror altogether.

DEVLIN You leave? What will I do? How will I cope? Go on then, leave. It's a free country.

MANSFIELD gets up to go. But for some reason doesn't walk out. Just leans against bar, drops his head.

No. No. Maybe leavin's not such a good idea, hey Terence? Out there? Ooh, I can feel the chill already. Hear that hollow ring. No love out there, is there boy? Nothin' out there but a big old cold house. A big old cold Da. And a dead mother. Better the Devlin you know, eh?

MIKEY *and* **JOE** *laugh at this.* **MANSFIELD** *sits down, deflated.*

Now. C'mon. Let's practice. When he comes in, what do we say?

JOE "Good afternoon, Mr. Black. And how are you today?"

MIKEY Shut up dipshit.

DEVLIN No Mikey. He's right. That's exactly what we say. "Good afternoon, Mr. Black. How are you today? Sit the fuck down you rich bastard." *(beat)* Mikey – that's when you get up off your prissy little behind and stop pretendin' you're a fucken cripple.

JOE But he is a fucken cripple. A fucken mental cripple.

DEVLIN *(to* **JOE***)* Shut up! *(to* **MIKEY***)* You get up and close the door. You bolt it. Do it now. So we see. *(pause)* Get up!

MIKEY *gets up. Limps to the door. Bolts upper bolt and lower bolts, locks the door – there is a key already in it – he takes this out.*

No. Don't lock it.

MIKEY Why not?

DEVLIN If we need to get out fast then we don't want messin' with keys, right? Leave the key in and leave it unlocked.

MIKEY Right. *(unlocks the door)* OK? **(MIKEY** *limps back to where he was sitting)*

DEVLIN OK. **(MIKEY** *sits down)* Forgettin' somethin'?

MIKEY What?

DEVLIN How's he goin' to get in if the door's bolted? When. He. Comes. Back. From. Tote. "Er – excuse me Mr. Black, while we – the hoodlums currently robbin' your pub – open the front door for ya. And no, DON'T run and get the cops while we're doin' it. Please! Oh pleeeease!" Jesus fuck, Mikey. Use yer loaf.

MIKEY *gets up, unbolts the door, hobbles back.*

MIKEY Right. No bolts. He's presently free ta enter.

DEVLIN Then Joe, you reassure Mr Black. Put him at his ease. Persuade him ta – quietly and calmly – tell us where he's hidden the stash we reckon he has. *(***JOE** *makes a punch move into his own hand)* He will say he has buck-all of course. But that's where you come in, Terence. You explain how we've come to the conclusion he's lyin'. How we know he's a stash of money hidden somewhere. How we've mathematically worked it out.

MANSFIELD I tell him I know who he is. He's a big time gambler. Big reputation. Cash bets, every day. There's money in the till but not much. He hasn't much of a life, he's no wife. Has few other expenses. Oh – and – he's careless: leaves his pub open. All of which points to a particular behavioural profile, a personality profile in keeping… *(***JOE** *and* **MIKEY** *laugh at this)*

JOE Personality profile! Wouldya go up er that! You're a fucken queer bastard Terry Mansfield.

MANSFIELD Shut your mouth Joe or I'll kill your dog. You hear me you thick cunt?

JOE *is silenced by the swiftly delivered retort, by the venom in* **MANSFIELD***'s tone.*

Pause.

We tell Prentice Black that such behaviour suggests a particular kind of personality. A man with money who doesn't seem to care much about it. Might even have some of it upon the premises. Cash that we would prefer he donated to us, instead of Tote. Immediately.

DEVLIN *claps.*

DEVLIN Well said. Well said. Eloquent in fact. That's exactly which way it should go. No blood. No punches. And try to keep 'fuck' out of yezer mouths for one fucken minute *(they laugh)*. Keep it clean. Short and sweet. Bolt the door behind him. Take a friendly approach. Make him a cup a tea, give him a biscuit. Talk about his problems. But most importantly, find the location of that cash.

MIKEY What if he has none?

DEVLIN What? Biscuits? (**JOE** *and* **DEVLIN** *laugh*)

MIKEY What I mean is Dev, what if this whole stakeout shit's a pointless exercise?

DEVLIN You been watchin' too many films, Mikey. We're just waitin'. That's all. Waitin' and seein'. And then we'll know if he's lyin'. I'll know. Spent my whole life with you lyin' scumbags, I'll fucking know.

MIKEY And if he's tellin' the truth – and he's nothin'?

DEVLIN Well, then we'll leave. Easy. We'll walk out. He'll not say a thing about us after we leave here, I guarantee that.

MANSFIELD How d'you know?

There is commotion outside the door. We hear **PRENTICE BLACK** *outside, laughing. He opens door, hangs back to talk to someone passing. An unintelligible, good-humoured banter. Or – we hear some, or all, of what* **PRENTICE** *says:*

"Go on home, **JIMMY**. *Give that money to your wife! Keep outta the place! Fucken mug's game, I'm tellin' ya."*

DEVLIN Just fucken watch me now Terry – and I'll learn ya! *(opens and closes his knife then puts it in his pocket)*

They spread out around the door. Door opens. **MIKEY** *slides in behind it. Once* **PRENTICE** *is inside,* **MIKEY** *bolts the door behind him – bolting top and bottom.*

DEVLIN *and* **MANSFIELD** *stand.* **JOE** *jumps up from behind the bar.*

JOE Good afternoon, Mr. Black. And how are you today?

Blackout.

Scene Four

PRENTICE BLACK is reclining in a chair, centre-stage, smoking. He is dressed in a suit, white shirt and braces. The jacket of his suit is around his chair. The others are sitting casually around him, attentively listening. JOE *is sitting up on the bar, swinging his legs.*

PRENTICE Then I was with my wee niece going North and we give this business-lookin' fella a lift. He's hitchin', side of the road. All dickyed up, suit and tie. He gets in the car and we're driving along and my wee niece, she's only young, seventeen like, wee girl like, she asks him what's in his briefcase and he tells her, ya know, to goway and mind her own fucking business. "Mind your own fucking business", he says. "Mind your own *fucking* business". Well ya know I'm thinking that's a bit much. Mean, she's only a wee girl. So then, anyways, I leave him at the Carrickdale and says to him "that's it". "That's as far as we go". So he gets out. Shirty kind of fella. Ya know the type. And we're only half a mile down the road, niece and me, when she sees he's gone and left the briefcase behind him in the seat. Jesus. So we pull over – and sure – what else? What would anyone do? What would you do? Course you would. She opens it.

Pause.

JOE And what was in it? Jesus!

MIKEY Guns I'd say. Guns and fucken money.

JOE Fucken semtex, man. That's how she's comin' now, man. Out in the open. Bags, briefcases. In your face.

MANSFIELD Porno I'd say.

DEVLIN Well come on! What was in the case, man?

PRENTICE *(wags his finger at them.)* Mind your own fucking business. *(laughs)*

MIKEY Good one Prentice.

PRENTICE *(laughing)* By the short and curlies there boy, huh?

DEVLIN Aye. Aye.

PRENTICE Come on, we'll have a song.

> **PRENTICE** *sings. As song* progresses the others join in – half enthused by, half mocking* **PRENTICE**.
>
> THE WIND WAS RISING.
> AND THE DAY DECLINING
> AS I LAY PINING IN MY PRISON CELL
> AND THAT AULD TRIANGLE
> WENT JINGLE JANGLE
> ALONG THE BANKS OF THE ROYAL CANAL.
>
> **JOE** *claps, slaps the bar-top, 'ya-hooh', mock-Irish 'getting into the session' behaviour. This gets everyone going – except* **DEVLIN** *– who indicates to the others to be quiet.*

DEVLIN Now. Prentice. 'Bout that other thing. Why don't ya talk us through it again?

PRENTICE *(angry)* Look, what part of nothin' do ya not get lads? *(beat)* Here you *(to* **MANSFIELD***)*, I know your face. Don't I know you? Mansfield. You his son? Mansfield's son? The solicitor?

JOE Aye. They used ta own the Derryhale. *(***DEVLIN** *clips* **JOE** *around the head for this reveal)*

PRENTICE You his son? *(***MANSFIELD** *does not answer)* You are. Recognise ya from the paper.

---

* *The Auld Triangle* is a song by Brendan Behan. It makes its first appearance in *The Quare Fellow* and has since become a popular song in pubs. I have also heard it sung by the crowd at anti-austerity marches in Dublin.

DEVLIN Paper? What ya done this time, Terry?

MANSFIELD You said no names.

PRENTICE Don't worry about bloody names. Know yez all anyway. Seen yez around.

DEVLIN What paper?

PRENTICE The sister's graduation. She's gone on for Medicine.

DEVLIN Never told us about that now, Terry, did ya?

MANSFIELD What's it to you?

DEVLIN Don't speak to me like that in front of the guests, Terence, please.

PRENTICE Good-lookin'.

MIKEY That the blonde one?

PRENTICE That's it.

DEVLIN One with glasses?

PRENTICE No glasses in paper. She looked nice.

DEVLIN You hold her glasses while...

MANSFIELD She only wears them for reading.

MIKEY I'd do her with or without.

JOE I fucken wouldn't. Looks like a right stuck up bitch with those glasses. Wouldn't go near her. Not even with your cock.

MIKEY She wouldn't go near you either in case she contaminated her brain-cells with stupidness. *(**MIKEY** makes masturbation moves with his hand)*

JOE Fuck off cripple.

DEVLIN You doin' her then, Terence?

JOE AND MICKEY Wooh!

JOE Look, he's gone all red. Opened the can of family worms there, Dev.

MIKEY No he hasn't. Terry don't like bints, 'n that right Ter? Not even when they're related. Not even when they've graduated from Medicine College or whatever they call it in your world.

MANSFIELD Royal College of Surgeons. She's a surgeon.

JOE Wooh!

DEVLIN Likes the knife then?

MANSFIELD She's good at it. Don't know what she likes.

DEVLIN Bit like her brother, then. Good with knives.

Pause.

See, you don't know – no, you have no fucking clue, Mr. Black, what you are dealin' with here.

PRENTICE Big boys. Yeah.

DEVLIN Between us, there is, how shall I say, a wealth of experience in the cuttin'-up-limbs department. In the punchin' and stabbin' and shite-kickin' department. Not somethin' we actually set out to do, is it lads?

JOE No, I fucken hate blood I do.

MIKEY Likewise.

DEVLIN Just somethin' that seems to happen.

PRENTICE Yeah. Yeah. I read you perfectly. *(he stands)* Now. We've had our fun. Been patient with yez – so time to go, eh? Time for yez all to get out of my pub. Been hospitable enough I think.

DEVLIN *(steely)* Sit the fuck down.

Long pause. **PRENTICE** *sits.*

PRENTICE Could I –

DEVLIN What?

PRENTICE A drink of water. Please. Out of me own pub like. If yez wouldn't mind.

    DEVLIN *clicks his fingers.*

DEVLIN Joe, water for the man please. Ice?

PRENTICE No.

DEVLIN No ice, Joe. And hurry up about it. (**JOE** *gives glass of water to* **MIKEY** *who brings it over to* **PRENTICE** *in the chair.*) Now. We don't want to take all day, Prentice. We've had a long night of it and we all need to go home and get some sleep.

MIKEY Yeah, spit it out, Prentice. I need to get out of here. See my girl.

PRENTICE You should just get jobs. *(all huff and puff at this)* Lot of yez. Big world out there. Plenty of avenues open ta yez. What are yez at with me? I worked hard in my life.

    DEVLIN *goes mental at this, grabs the glass of water, smashes it, throws a stool and smashes a lot of bottles at the back of the bar.*

DEVLIN Pissin' me off old man.

MANSFIELD Jonah leave it.

PRENTICE Jonah?

DEVLIN Don't use my name in front of the cunt, all right?

PRENTICE Jonah Devlin's boy. You must be.

DEVLIN What do you know about jobs? About needin' one, not havin' one? Huh? Huh?

PRENTICE They're there if you look.

DEVLIN My oul fella –

PRENTICE Jonah Devlin is it?

DEVLIN Know what that bastard in the hotel said to him, *(points across the way)* there, last week? Up for interview he was. Down to the last five for assistant doorman. Know what the fucker asked him do? Asked him clean the fucking bog. So he could 'watch him and see'.

PRENTICE Ah Quinn's always cut corners. Squeezes two jobs from one. I'm sorry for Jonah. *(beat)* Spent too long fuckin' around Belfast but, know what I'm sayin' kid?

DEVLIN It's abuse that is. Fucken slaves they want. Quinn took advantage of my da's position.

PRENTICE He left Christine alone often enough, did Jonah.

DEVLIN Shut up about her. You shut up about her.

PRENTICE Sure. Sure. No problem. But I'm sure you won't mind me saying she was a beauty in her day. Your mother. Maytime Festival Queen. None could hold a candle to her that year. Bright too. Eatin' out of her hand they were. Worked in here that time, ya know that? Barmaid. Most gracious in the place. She never tell you all the stories I told her about Africa, boy?

DEVLIN Ma's too busy to be talkin' ta me about your oul back-in-the-day, Prentice.

PRENTICE Well, she was a good listener, Christine. Always seemed like she was.

JOE Never said your Ma worked in *The Congo*, Dev?

DEVLIN First I heard of it.

PRENTICE She didn't stay long.

DEVLIN Why's that?

PRENTICE Pregnant that's why. Here three months then off to waste her life on you. Poor girl.

MIKEY Thought you said you never been in here before, Dev?

JOE Yeah Dev. You were. All snug inside yer Ma, like a little kangaroo.

DEVLIN Shut the fuck up about it all right? Shut up. Shut up.

Long pause.

PRENTICE You sure you're not runnin' some kinda protection scam here? Is that what this is? Because the boys do leave me alone. Jonah knows that. I know them all. Big Cat MacInteggart included. I been political. I seen a lot a shit.

DEVLIN No such thing as protection on offer here, Prentice.

PRENTICE All right. Well, I see what you're sayin': yez are fine upstandin' young fellas let down by society and the times that are in it. Nice work if ya can get it and all that jazz.

MIKEY He's bein' patronisin'.

MANSFIELD We need to move on now, Dev. Come on, man. People will want to come in.

PRENTICE But the times will get better in this country. You'll see. How it'll all change. Everyone gainfully employed. No need to envy a man like me. Things will evolve. With prosperity. That's what happens. I mean it's the law of probability. Our turn will come. All this can't go on forever, a decade of gloom, young fellas robbin' grannies. Read there last week – family held up in the town for a van. Imagine that. Held hostage in your own home for a fucken van? Didn't even belong to the fella. Works for Maguire's Furniture, he does. Well, you go to America, ta towns like this, ya see vans everyplace. Prosperity. Every man looked after. *(beat)* Look, take what's in the till why don't ya, and fuck off home. I don't mind. I'll say nothin'.

JOE D'ya think we're stupid? *(holds the money up that was in the till)*

DEVLIN All seventeen quid of it?

PRENTICE Take the whiskey and wine then. Cellar full a the stuff. Get money for that up North, if you don't drink it. Or maybe sell to Mansfield's father. He'll buy it.

ALL – *except* **MANSFIELD** – *laugh.*

JOE Good idea, oul fella.

PRENTICE *(to* **MANSFIELD***)* Ah, only jokin' boy. *(Beat.)* You shouldn't be here though. What you doin' with them? Yez are all Grange lads, am I right? That's a fucking sewer anyways.

DEVLIN *laughs mockingly – long and hard – at this. The others join in.*

DEVLIN Oh, he's a great sense of humour, don't you agree lads? For an oul coffin dodger. First thing I look for in a person actually: a sense of humour. I go up to them and say: "have you a sense of humour, cunt?" And if they say: "yes, I do, as a matter of fact, have a sense of humour", I know then I'm in good company.

MIKEY Ya'd need a sense a humour in this kip.

DEVLIN But jokin' aside now Grandda: where's the money? **(PRENTICE** *gives* **DEVLIN** *a 'fuck you' look,* **DEVLIN** *grabs him by the hair.)* Where's the fucking money? *(takes a breath. Beat)* Maybe it's time you explain, Tolstoy, hmmm? Your turn. Explain to the man what his behavioural 'profile' – or whatever the fuck you call it – is leadin' us to believe about him.

MANSFIELD *stands, prepares himself.*

Pause.

MANSFIELD You win today, Prentice?

PRENTICE No. Came back didn't I?

MANSFIELD Bet on the big race?

PRENTICE Aye.

MANSFIELD What d'you bet?

PRENTICE Evens on some nag.

MANSFIELD You go to the bank?

PRENTICE No.

MANSFIELD You just used the till money in Tote.

PRENTICE Yeah. A little. Ya know.

MANSFIELD No use for banks. If it's not in the till it's under the bed, the mattress maybe.

PRENTICE No! I… OK, look, I see where yer goin'. OK, I went to the bank. This morning. With yesterday's takings. The most of it.

MANSFIELD You sure about that?

PRENTICE Yeah. I remember now. To make the deposit.

MANSFIELD And you got money *out* to go gambling. Like a float sorta. When you went there.

PRENTICE Aye. Like a float, aye.

MANSFIELD But why bother with the bank, Prentice, if you were going gambling, huh? Or – maybe – you went to the bank, like you said, with the till-money, the most of it, because – *you didn't need it*. Because – you already *had* a float. A stash. In an old coat, shoe, biscuit tin. My old fella does that. I reckon you were coming for more outta that *stash*, just there,* when you came in. What d'ya say ta that?

****JOE** *has been taking pictures off the wall and dropping them.* **PRENTICE** *looks over.*

PRENTICE Leave the fucken pictures will ya?

JOE 'Morrocco 1957'. Looks like Tommy Cooper. Hey Dev, doesn't he look like Tommy Cooper? "Just like that. He-he-he."

JOE practices his Tommy Cooper hand movements. He, **MIKEY** *and* **DEVLIN** *snigger at this.*

PRENTICE It's called a fez, you imbecile.

DEVLIN Get back to the money, Terry.

JOE suddenly jumps over the bar towards **PRENTICE**.

JOE Just. Like. Fucken. That. You. Fuck.

JOE lashes out and punches **PRENTICE** *in the face, rips off* **PRENTICE**'s *braces, and proceeds to tie him to the chair.*

MANSFIELD *(to* **DEVLIN***)* Call the gorilla off him will ya?

JOE Calling *me* a gorilla? Ya long-haired student drip.

DEVLIN *(to* **JOE***)* Tie him tight. Then over to the bar with ya.

JOE finishes tying **PRENTICE**, *moves away.* **MANSFIELD** *resumes his questioning.*

MANSFIELD Who were ya talking ta outside, Prentice?

PRENTICE A friend. A friend who'll be here in five minutes if I'm not in Tote for the next race. He'll come over and raise ructions when he sees this. You know what I've seen in my life? Know what I've been through? All the things. Don't need this oul tripe, I tell ya.

DEVLIN When yer friend comes, the pub will be closed and you'll be quiet. He'll think you're asleep. We'll make sure he thinks it. Now, looks like you're caught out with your story, Mr. Black. So if I were you I'd quit while I was ahead.

PRENTICE No class, lot of yez. No breeding. All scum. Even you Mansfield. All of ya. Scum. Scum from the slum.

DEVLIN 'Scum from the slum'. He's a poet and he didn't know it.

MICKEY AND JOE Wooh! Look at him.

JOE Ya look like stuffed steak in those braces.

MIKEY Aye. We could almost eat ya.

PRENTICE When have youse ever seen steak boys, huh? Fray Bentos is all youse seen I'd fucken say.

MANSFIELD Now, wait. Let me explain something to ya, Mr. Black.

DEVLIN All right. You can quit now, Terry. Said yer piece. Enough.

MANSFIELD One second. You *(to **PRENTICE**)* talk about class as if it were a good thing to have. "God, she's a class bit of stuff, the sister, boy" – or "you're a wanton boy Mansfield with no class at all, bejaysus" – and so on – *(the others laugh).* You think you recognise it because you have it, isn't that it? After all, you're a big-shot businessman. Way above us plebs. But you've no right to use a word like that. Not in that way. Not when you are making a living out of other people's weaknesses. Or maybe I'm wrong: perhaps you turn away the drunk on his twenty-fifth pint.

JOE Like fuck he does.

MANSFIELD Which makes him what?

MIKEY A drug-dealin' ponce.

DEVLIN A pusher. That's what you are, Mr. Black. A pusher.

MANSFIELD Capitalist pig's what he is. What people like him are called in my college. Capitalist pigs. These pigs think they are a 'class' above. I mean what are pubs? Drug dens. What are bookies?

JOE Drug dens.

MANSFIELD Truth is, Prentice, you and others like you, are no better than us. And you've no more class either.

JOE And he's moanin'. Keepin' us waitin'. Because we want a few skileetoes. Us poor young fellas with no jobs.

DEVLIN Whose father's pride is crushed from bog cleanin' requests.

MIKEY I've a job.

JOE Listen to the milky bar kid. Clearin' out horse-shite's not a job.

PRENTICE *(to **MANSFIELD**)* Your mother checked out of yer life quick enough, didn't she? Must have known the misery she'd given birth ta.

MANSFIELD Keeping up with the likes of you was what was wrong with her, Mr. Black. Made her sick. That's all she 'checked out' for. Keeping up with the Jones' and the flashing-their-cash-in-the-middle-of-a-fucking-recession Prentice Blacks of this town.

PRENTICE Was always unhappy. Like she was suckin' a lemon most days. Now I know why.

MANSFIELD Every unhappy family is unhappy in its own way.

PRENTICE Who said that?

MANSFIELD Tolstoy.

JOE That's you lanky.

MIKEY It's the writer he's named after, dipshit.

PRENTICE Well she deserved better 'n you with your thug Grange buddies, tell ya that. Came from a good family she did. Lovely people. Genteel. Bad day she met your father. He'd a driven anyone to it.

DEVLIN Now that's not nice talk, is it Mr. Black? Poor Mansfield. No more Ma. How would you like it, huh? Your darlin' Ma foun' swingin' from the ceilin' by her own shoelaces.

DEVLIN *has now brought all attention back to himself. Long pause. Lights up a cigarette, walks up to* **PRENTICE** *in the chair.*

The Congo. Why'd you go callin' the place a strange fucken name the like a that, huh? After some far-off land in Africa.

MIKEY Because it's dark and full of blood-suckin' insects in here, that's why.

DEVLIN Come on, Prentice. Talk.

MANSFIELD He was out there. That's why.

DEVLIN So he says.

JOE Shoulda stayed.

PRENTICE How could I stay there? Place erupted. That was that.

DEVLIN Doin' what in Africa exactly?

Pause.

PRENTICE Excavating.

MIKEY Were ya one of those 'archaeologist' fellas?

JOE *(to* **MIKEY***)* Ya swatty bastard.

MANSFIELD He raped the place of diamonds and gold. Isn't that right, Mr. Black?

PRENTICE What I traded in! It was my job! Company I worked for were – excavating – or – if you prefer, mining. Copper, tin, diamonds. Then we were trading. When war broke, it broke big-time. Belgians realised what they'd given away, see: all that fucking wealth.

King Leopold, he's the one started it all, last century. Made the Congo his private little cash cow, sucking up all that wealth ta build Brussels. Anyway. Time I was there they decided to give it back. The Belgians. Until the likes of De Beers and Union Miniere started breathin' down their necks. Well, it looked like they were goin' back on the deal. And it didn't go down too well with the natives. They went ape-shit. Tribe on tribe. Kinda like here with the civil war. Same old shit, ya know. Anyway… I came back here in '62. But what had changed? Not much fucken better. Few years later: Sunningdale, soldiers on the border, scumbags like you. I had Republican sympathies in the early days. Sure me and Jonah were. *(beat)* Ah… to answer your question: when I opened this place I wanted to remind people of how easy it is to lose what ya have. The name – was a symbol of all that for me. Of how easy it is when you're not vigilant, for someone to come inta your land, inta your peacefulness, and plunder it off ya wholesale.

DEVLIN Yeah. But you did the plunderin' them days.

PRENTICE Yep. I did.

DEVLIN Take any of those Congo diamonds home with ya? Any of that African gold, maybe?

PRENTICE What I took is long gone. You're standin' in it.

DEVLIN But ya took stuff?

PRENTICE Souvenirs as you can see. Some drums. Some pictures. Some ivory, to my great shame, which I gave away.

DEVLIN Have ya any diamonds here, Mr. Black?

PRENTICE No.

DEVLIN Well I'd say that's a mighty comedown, wouldn't ya boys? One day diamonds and Africa, a thousand acres of sky and sunshine…

JOE … and the next, held hostage by a bunch of cunts in a border shithole. Aye, that's a fall the size of… Victoria Falls. *(a cocksure glance at **MIKEY** for knowing this geographical detail)* A long, long way.

PRENTICE How is it a fall? To come here? Home? You think life anywhere else – "life at the top", "life in the sun" – is better than here? Maybe. But not much.

JOE Oh fuck that.

PRENTICE Yez don't know your history. Of here, or there. Of nowhere I'd say. All is a blank slate up there with youze. Dangerous that.

DEVLIN He loves the bloody history lessons.

PRENTICE You're only kids! Fledglings! Youze think this is it? No jobs – end of the world? No. You'll get to the end of the world many times in yezer lives and it won't be to do with jobs or money. There'll be bigger things. You take it from me.

DEVLIN We've lived Prentice. We've lived twice what you done at our age.

PRENTICE Oh, ya think so?

DEVLIN We got hard here. This shithole did that to us.

PRENTICE It's no differ than any other town. You'll learn. So long as there's people in places, nowhere is unique. It's dross, aye, but it's our dross. We're here, ain't we? We should take care, and live deep. Before it's too late.

JOE Where else you been, Granda?

PRENTICE Most places. I been to them all. *(Pause)* Listen, I – I can get to the bank. There's time. Just tell me how much you want.

DEVLIN No fucken banks. No outside. No people. Just – in here. You got valuables, souvenirs, diamonds – or don't ya?

PRENTICE I said you're standin' in it. This is my only diamond left.

DEVLIN I'm gettin' a warm, tinglin' sorta feeling makes me think you might be lyin' about that Prentice.

Beat.

PRENTICE You? You warm? I know you. I know your type. You're cold. And you'll always be cold. Colder than five years down a mine. Colder than the first night alone, after the woman you've loved thirty years has died. Colder than the morgue. Colder than hell.

DEVLIN Upstairs! Get him upstairs!

Blackout.

Scene Five

MIKEY *and* **MANSFIELD** *at the dartboard.*

MICKEY Goin' out tonight?

MANSFIELD Might just do that. You?

MICKEY Yeah. Bloody right I am.

MANSFIELD Yeah? Where you goin'? Clubbin'?

MICKEY Fuck clubbin'. Old birds that's for. Old slappers and diesel queens.

MANSFIELD Maybe I'll go where you are.

MIKEY You won't! I'm takin' my girl out you wee bastard.

> **MANSFIELD** *throws three darts. All hit the edge of the board. He checks where his feet are positioned.*

Easy knowin' you at college. Your head in your books. Not on important things like – *(throws a dart)* double *(throws a dart)* bulls eye! Hey. Twenty five for me you cunt. *(**MIKEY** writes score on the board)*

Screams heard from upstairs. Smashed glasses, a rumble, **DEVLIN**'*s voice. Angry and fast. Then* **JOE**'*s manic laughter, followed by three loud smacks and more screams.*

Silence.

MANSFIELD Where you drink with her? Where you drink with your girl?

MIKEY She's from the country. Go up her way. Coffin Bridge. Out the border way. Des's place.

MANSFIELD Country girl?

MIKEY Aye. A teacher.

MANSFIELD Of what, milking cows?

MIKEY You fucker. Substitute teacher. National school. She's clever.

MANSFIELD You getting married?

MICKEY Maybe, yeah.

MANSFIELD I'd say so. By the sound of it.

MIKEY Tell ya what, this shit's no good anymore. Don't even fucken care about the money, do you?

MANSFIELD It's the principle though. That's what it's all about really.

MIKEY Principle? Devlin wouldn't know one of those if it bit him on the arse. Hey, keep behind the line here, see.

He moves **MANSFIELD** *back behind the line.*

MANSFIELD Well, he wastes his money, Prentice. And Devlin's dad is poor.

MIKEY His dad is a cunt. *(more screams from upstairs)* And the apple doesn't fall far from the tree, as they say…

MANSFIELD How's your foot?

MIKEY *(laughs)* Cut right through. Doesn't know what he's at, Joe. What you expect from a barber?

MANSFIELD Wouldn't let Joe near my fucken hair.

MIKEY Place closed down he was in. *(beat)* Da always says he has two sons and a barber.

MANSFIELD Three of yez then?

MIKEY Aye. Other in London. Nothin' for chippies here now.

DEVLIN *(off/upstairs)* Hey Mikey! Get up here. Tell Tolstoy watch the door. Tell him stay down. Probably faint if he came up.

JOE *laughs (off).*

MIKEY Right. *(gathers up the darts, tidies up, rubs out numbers from blackboard)* This is the outer-ring, right? Your aim is wide. Go closer. You can practice while we look for this fucken stash I doubt's there at all. Sounds like he's been kicked sideways already. He'd tell if he knew. *(walks towards door for upstairs. Stalls)* Ah fuck it. Let Dev wait. *(long pause. Lights up a cigarette)* We went to see this cottage ya know? Girl and me. Foothills of Omeath.

MANSFIELD Yeah? When was that?

MIKEY Sunday.

MANSFIELD Sunday?

MIKEY Aye. You can see the bay from this place. Brought her there on the back of my bike. She didn't mind, like. She's clever and has ambitions for herself. For me too, but I like that about her. Not like the ordinary oul rags Joe and me are used to hangin' out with. No, a lady. That's what Ma says. Anyway, we walked around this cottage. Old-style. Whitewashed. All the turf netted neatly by a shed. Long it was too, with a brook runnin' alongside it. And fuchsia. A whole bank of fuchsia. House was rightly small though, but enough, ya know? Two of us. She didn't say anythin' when I mentioned maybe we'd rent it if we could. She annoyed me then. We had a row and, well I... well I can't fuck it up, Mansfield. She's a lady. Not this time. Not her. Tonight's the night. Settle it. Move on, ya know? No more a this shit. That's it. That's fucken it.

Beat.

MANSFIELD He said one more adventure three times already.

MIKEY Aye.

DEVLIN *(off)* Mikey! *(beat)* Joe, get that brother of yours up here.

MIKEY Fuck this.

Exit **MIKEY**. **MANSFIELD** *practices his aim. There is a knock on the door.* **MANSFIELD** *panics, picks up bar stool, holds as a weapon.*

Silence.

Another knock. Sounds of **DEVLIN** *and* **JOE** *scrambling down the stairs.*

DEVLIN *and* **JOE** *enter. They have blood and white feathers all over their hands.*

DEVLIN Don't fucken answer it.

MANSFIELD I wasn't going ta.

As **DEVLIN** *comes closer,* **MANSFIELD** *sees the mess of blood on him.*

What's going on? What's that?

JOE *sticks up his hands, also bloody.*

JOE Been 'excavating'. *(sniggers)* Isn't that right, Dev? Been gettin' down and dirty in the ruby mines. *(laughs)*

Another knock.

MANSFIELD Oh Chrissake, what yez done?!

DEVLIN Go to the fucking window, you queer. Slow, slow, slow.

MANSFIELD *stands on the seat, peeps out the window.* **DEVLIN** *and* **JOE** *stand either side of the door.*

MANSFIELD Fuck! It's Gascy!

DEVLIN *goes to the door, unbolts and opens it. Pulls* **GASCOIGNE** *in, bolts door behind him.*

DEVLIN Fuck sake man!

MANSFIELD What ya doing, Gascy?

JOE Lookin' deadly, Gascy! Fucken deadly. Your hair. It's all...

GASCOIGNE Got noo jacket too.

DEVLIN Did ya fella?

GASCOIGNE Aye. Like your one now, Dev, so it iz.

DEVLIN Sure you're my fucken twin now, Gascy!

GASCOIGNE Yeaaaaah!!!!

JOE Like the linin', Dev.

DEVLIN What is it Joe, Tartan?

JOE *(checks jacket)* Some fucken check shit.

DEVLIN Silk or polyester?

JOE *(reads label, his bloody hands held out delicately)* Lining: 100% polyester. Still.

DEVLIN Still.

MANSFIELD How'd you know we were here, Gascy, huh?

GASCOIGNE I... I seen yez stop in the car. And I watched. And yez never came back.

DEVLIN That was ages ago.

GASCOIGNE I... I was gettin' the jacket, Dev. For the pub, like.

JOE Well, ya give us a big oul fucken fright there, Gascy.

GASCOIGNE Did I, Joe? Haaaaaa! *(sniggers)*

DEVLIN And no one else saw ya?

GASCOIGNE No way!

DEVLIN You fucken sure about that?

GASCOIGNE You betcha!

DEVLIN What about your Ma?

Beat.

GASCOIGNE I didn't bring her, Dev. No way.

DEVLIN Because she's a what, Gascy?

Beat.

GASCY A fucken cunt biddy bitch.

DEVLIN Aye. Good. Now. Let me look at ya. See that – is what I call – proper sartorial elegance. Better known as – a real cool fucken jacket.

Blackout.

Scene Six

Upstairs, the bedroom. Spartan space – but suggestive of the travels of Prentice Black. A double bed, radio on small bedside cupboard. A built-in wardrobe, a sideboard with upturned photos. Large map of Africa in the shape of Patrice Lumumba's head on the back wall. A gas fire, a few gas cylinders, a barrel along wall. Curtains fully drawn. Central bare bulb. Upturned bedside lamp. Some busted pillows, feathers everywhere. Darkness. **GASCOIGNE** *is being led into the room by* **DEVLIN**, *who has his hands around his eyes.* **JOE** *puts on the light (60 Watt).* **PRENTICE BLACK** *in an armchair, centre-stage, blood on his face, chest and legs, feathers stuck to him.* **DEVLIN** *takes his hands off* **GASCOIGNE**. **MANSFIELD** *slumps against wall, starts to cry.* **MIKEY** *goes up to* **JOE**, *wants him to leave, but* **JOE** *sizes up to him with* **DEVLIN**'s *knife.* **MIKEY** *backs off.*

DEVLIN If we knew you wanted to play some more, Gascy, we'd have let ya come with us, wouldn't we, Joe?

JOE Gascy's Mammy would worry though, eh Gascy?

DEVLIN You tell her where ya were last night, boy?

> **GASCOIGNE** *shakes his head.*

Good then. That's a good boy.

MIKEY What I tell ya about knives, Devlin, eh? He's *(meaning* **JOE***)* had warnings. *(to* **JOE***)* Too enthusiastic last time, eh Joe? Da will fucken blind ya when he gets ya now. No more knives he said. He give you that?

DEVLIN Who the fuck is 'he'? He? Who 'he', pig?

MIKEY Dev please, yav gone too far here, eh? Look, you've even made rich boy sick. He's cryin'. Come on. We should go.

DEVLIN Stop fussin'. He's only scratched. Aren't ya Granda?

GASCOIGNE Hot in here Dev. Not nice. Nice breeze outside. Maybe go to seaside instead, huh?

JOE No Gascy. We got better things ta do than make sandcastles.

GASCOIGNE I like sandcastles! Please Joe.

DEVLIN Come on now, Gascy.

GASCOIGNE We make whole city of sandcastles. I – I do have a big bucket for that Dev. Red one. We make whole new town on the beach. Please Dev. You my angel. I'm scared in here. Man has blood. Man is scary coz he has blood.

MANSFIELD Dev likes to be scared though. Gives him a big thrill, Gascy.

DEVLIN Ya don't wanna play. Is that it Gascy?

GASCOIGNE I do Dev, I do.

DEVLIN We can have fun here. What you say we do the beach another day?

GASCOIGNE OK. Dev.

DEVLIN And then we'll make loadsa sandcastles. A whole country of sandcastles. All along the shore. How's about that?

GASCOIGNE OK. OK. Iz good. Yeah.

DEVLIN Joe, start making Gascy a little less scared, why don't ya? A little less scared of Prentice there.

> **JOE** *starts to make fun of* **PRENTICE** *in the chair; cuts up a pillow with a knife, throws some feathers on* **PRENTICE** *and makes the squawking sounds and movements of a chicken.* **GASCOIGNE** *joins in. The two circle* **PRENTICE**.

MANSFIELD Oh man. Oh man.

MIKEY Fucking hell.

> **MIKEY** *turns away.* **MANSFIELD** *buries his head in his hands.* **JOE** *and* **GASCOIGNE** *carry on throwing handfuls of feathers at* **PRENTICE** *and occasionally at each other.*

DEVLIN See lads? Few oul scratches. Course, there'd be none at all if he told us where he's hidden it. *(to* **PRENTICE***)* Where've you hidden it, capitalist pig? *(to* **MANSFIELD***)* Hey. Hey, you. You want to take it from there?

MANSFIELD *(head still buried in his hands)* You're a sadist Devlin.

DEVLIN What was that? *(no answer)* What was that you queer cunt?

MANSFIELD You. Are. A fucking. Sadist.

> *Pause.*

DEVLIN Get up! Get up I said!

> **MANSFIELD** *stands by wall.* **DEVLIN** *goes up to him, slips both arms across* **MANSFIELD***'s neck, squashes his body right up against* **MANSFIELD***'s – pushes him against the wall.*

Say that to my fucking face, cunt.

> **MANSFIELD** *says nothing.*

Say it!

> **MANSFIELD** *turns his face to one side and groans.*

I tell you lads he's talking all right. Just not with his lips.

JOE What's he sayin'?

DEVLIN Let me see. He's sayin': "Ooh you are awful but I like ya".

JOE cracks up, followed by **GASCOIGNE**. **MIKEY** *grabs the knife (***DEVLIN***'s) off* **JOE**, *rushes over to* **PRENTICE BLACK**, *points it at his throat.*

MIKEY D'ya see fucker? *(all surprised at* **MIKEY** *suddenly taking the lead)* It's anarchy in here. Gone-to-fuck, see? Chaos, pure and simple. *(to the lads)* What he say he had? Anythin'? Has he anythin'?

JOE He let somethin' slip. Talked about some box with ivory on.

MIKEY Right. So he's got a box. Tell us where the fucken box is, Prentice. NOW you stupid old man. See what you got in here? A retard, a psycho, a sadist and a fucking queer. See what you got? No hope, that's what you got. Think you stand a chance with this lot? I'm your only hope. I've got a job, a girl, a life to go home ta. You tell me where that fucken box is or I'll kill you myself.

PRENTICE *moans at this. Rubs his lips together.*

Water? *(***PRENTICE*** nods)* More water! Jesus! This guy's a fish. Water someone. *(no one moves. They look to each other)* Ya mean yez came up, battered him half to death and ya'd no water? Not very optimistic were yez? Want a man to spill his guts, ya need water. Fear dries the mouth, d'yez not know that by now? Rank fucken amateurs.

MANSFIELD I'll get it. *(exits, watched by* **DEVLIN***)*

DEVLIN You come straight back here, right?

Pause.

MIKEY *(to* **PRENTICE***)* You *like* fish?

DEVLIN Fish? What the fuck man?

MIKEY Answer me! Maybe you like sea-trout – or salmon, Prentice?

JOE Mikey goes fishin' every weekend, Dev. That's what he means. It's his favourite fucken subject.

PRENTICE *nods.*

MIKEY Both. OK. Good. Coz I can get you a life supply. Bring ya free fish every weekend. For what – for a year? For a year if ya want it. Two years? Until ya die. That is a good deal. Free food until you die.

DEVLIN *Free fucken food?* You think that's gonna make him talk? A load a fucken fish? Who d'ya think ya are? Jesus Christ?

MIKEY Free fish comin' ta the door every weekend is nothin' ta scoff at man! It's somethin' isn't it? An offer, an exchange. Prentice – that's your dinner sorted for the rest a yer life, man!

DEVLIN Well, hurry up there, Mikey, before I fucken fillet ya out with that knife.

MIKEY Listen Prentice. All ya have to do is give these scumbags the money. The stash. The box. I don't want a thing.

JOE Well yer not gettin' any of mine.

MIKEY Any of your what?

JOE Money!

MIKEY There isn't any yet ya silly cunt. There's seventeen quid split four ways.

DEVLIN Split five with Gascy.

MIKEY Four. I'm not in.

JOE He thinks he's special coz he's engaged to that bint.

MIKEY *(to* **JOE***)* Listen, when he tells us where that box is, that's it. We're goin'. That's you and me, Joe. Out the fuck, OK?

JOE Don't you fucken...

MIKEY Listen to me! You – are – comin' – with – me.

JOE Had-away-and-shite.

MIKEY And that's fucking it! We get the box, we get the money, we leave. You *(to* **PRENTICE***)* think about my offer... but after this you say nothin' to no one, ya hear?

DEVLIN We can't trust him to do that, Mikey.

MIKEY We have to!

DEVLIN No Mikey. We don't.

> **MIKEY** *stares at* **DEVLIN** *who gives him a particular 'cold' look.* **MANSFIELD** *enters with water, brings it over to* **PRENTICE** *– who drinks slowly, hand shaking.*

PRENTICE The box... the box is...

MIKEY No! No wait! *(to* **DEVLIN***)* What did you mean...

DEVLIN Out of the way now.

MIKEY No, no Prentice. Now, listen. I'm sorry. I *(looks at* **DEVLIN***)* – I changed my mind. Don't. Don't say it. Fuck the fish.

DEVLIN What ya doing?! Why'd ya butt in? Didn't ya just tell him ta... Who made you God?

MIKEY Who made you God?

DEVLIN You did, you fucking cunt.

MIKEY *(to* **PRENTICE***)* You say where that box is Prentice, I can't, what I'm sayin' is – I mean: look at him! *(referring to* **DEVLIN***).* Look at this! In here! I'm sorry. But I can't ensure… you better lay off him now, Dev. I'm fucken serious.

DEVLIN *moves in quickly, lifts* **PRENTICE** *off the chair by the throat, smacks him, threatens to do it again.*

DEVLIN Endgame. Now, where's the ivory box, Grandpa?

PRENTICE *(slurred)* Floorboard. Window.

Blackout.

Scene Seven

PRENTICE BLACK *is out of the chair, which has been flung to one side, and is lying on the floor, holding on to his stomach. The floorboards by the window have been pulled up. 'The box' is open and in* **DEVLIN**'s *hands. He twists the key at the side of the box and a tune is played:* Frère Jacques. **DEVLIN** *sings along (a phonetic pronunciation of the French)*

FRÈRE JACQUES, FRÈRE JACQUES,
DORMEZ-VOUS? DORMEZ-VOUS?
SONELEMATINA (FOR 'SONNEZ LES MATINES!')
SONELEMATINA (FOR 'SONNEZ LES MATINES!')
DING, DANG, DONG.
DING, DANG, DONG.

DEVLIN *takes the single note that was in the box and then shuts it.*

Ten pounds. A life for ten pounds. Not gonna look good in the papers is it?

MIKEY More 'n your da earned in a while I'd say. By the way, what is the price of semtex these days anyway?

DEVLIN *puts the money in his pocket, slowly lights up two cigarettes. He does not react (as expected) to* **MIKEY**'s *remark. He gives one cigarette to* **PRENTICE** *(lying on the floor) who – shakily – smokes it.*

DEVLIN What you know, Mikey? Nothin'. He has beliefs my Da. So? What can I do? Huh? My Ma – she works. She believes in him she does. Should see her sometimes. In late. All the guff she has ta listen ta. And she's been sick, ya know? We tell her, I tell her, don't go in, but she does. She believes in him, see. Not tuppence in his pocket but she never sees him miss a meetin'. There she is, standin' hours on end in that shop, veins poppin' out of her legs. Man, you should see the veins.

I see her in photos and there's a glamourous woman lookin' forward to somethin' in life. Maytime Festival Queen. And what does she get? Grim. That's what. Grim. He goes off givin' his speeches, his rallyin' cries. Kerry, Donegal, wherever. And who's paid for it? My Ma. My Ma and her lost dreams and her draggin' that wicker fucken trolley up and down this town. So you slag off my da and his choices Mikey, you make worse of my Ma and all she's believed in and sacrificed. And I don't like people slagging off my Ma.

Pause.

Now. What would you say, Terry? About Prentice here. At this stage in the proceedings. Huh? Is he holdin' out? The oul stubborn fella. Oul dead breath. D'ya reckon he's holdin' out?

Pause.

MANSFIELD *(gets up – reluctantly)* Prentice, come on now. You're enjoying the smoke aren't ya? Things looking up, yeah? Yeah. Well maybe you should tell us where you've hidden the float now, huh? The gambling money. Was that it, what was in that box? Not even I believe that it was. Listen man, you left the pub wide open. Hour at least. You're careless, Prentice. What were we supposed to think, eh? Have ya anything in here worth anything? *(to* **DEVLIN**) You tried his pockets in the wardrobe?

DEVLIN Nothin'. Sweet-wrappers, bettin' slips, pens. That's it.

MANSFIELD You're not playing smart sir. This could have been a lot – easier. *(beat)* Prentice? Prentice? Ah man. He's fucken out of it. We should go. This is fucking bad. Prentice? *(he grabs him)* Prentice. Where's the fucking money, man?

PRENTICE *groans.* **GASCOIGNE** *rushes up to* **PRENTICE** *and proceeds to piss on him. The others are stunned. They laugh (a hysterical/incredulous kind of laughter).*

What the fuck… oh, oh you stupid cunt!

JOE Don't call him that! That better, Gascy? That a relief? Yeah! He's a big oul bastard, isn't he?

GASCOIGNE *laughs his head off.*

GASCOIGNE He was on fire, Joe! I'm puttin' out the smoke. Wooh!

DEVLIN Oh, how we reel them in, Mikey eh? The new recruits. The little fishes. Next you'll be hangin' round the graveyard on the nightshift with us Prentice, won't you old man?

MANSFIELD Oh, you'll have him in there one way or another, I'd say.

JOE Ya know, that might not be a bad idea, Dev. And we'd have free booze, entertainin' back-in-the-day stories about Africa and Tommy Cooper hats…

DEVLIN About the days when ya'd nothing for Christmas only an oul orange.

MIKEY I'd say Prentice knows plenty of cops too.

MANSFIELD He stinks. Ah man. Can't go near him now.

JOE All those fucken bananas, Gascy. It must be.

MIKEY What we waitin' for? Someone is gonna come. This is a public house. He's gotta open sometime.

DEVLIN Well then we better finish this. Finish the whole thing and get goin'.

Pause.

Anyone check the back door? *(beat)* No. And why am I not surprised? *(**GASCOIGNE** moans and whispers to **JOE**)* What's with him?

JOE He wants the toilet.

DEVLIN He just had it!

JOE Worse than that. *(the others suddenly smell **GASCOIGNE**, wave off his smell)*

MIKEY Jesus Christ!

DEVLIN Take him then.

MANSFIELD I'll check downstairs.

DEVLIN No. You stay. I'll check. And when I come back, no more fuckin' about, right? *(to **PRENTICE**)* We'll tear this place up from top to bottom. *(to **MIKEY** and **MANSFIELD**)* Watch him. The old can be awful stubborn fuckers sometimes. *(exits)*

> **JOE** *takes* **GASCOIGNE** *next door to the toilet.* **MANSFIELD** *and* **MIKEY** *alone with* **PRENTICE** *who is now curled up on the floor.*

MANSFIELD He's hurt bad.

MIKEY This is mental.

> **MIKEY** *walks over to* **PRENTICE**, *looks him over.*

He stinks. *(to **MANSFIELD**)* Here. Have a hard man's cigarette.

They both light up.

Silence.

Them van fellas Prentice was on about. I know them. Done an eighty-year-old woman up the country too. Real scumbags.

MANSFIELD Thought they'd guns up the country.

MIKEY Some do. Some don't. *(pause)* They *are* cruel bastards generally, though, country bumpkins.

MANSFIELD Are they?

MIKEY They are.

MANSFIELD In what way?

MIKEY They don't give a fuck about animals that's for fucken sure. Farmers? They're like the worst people to be in charge a the countryside. I'm tellin' ya. Killers. Whole lot a them. Hunters. Hunt deer, like. Ever hear a deer cry when it's hunted?

MANSFIELD No.

MIKEY Go right through ya. Hits somethin'.

MANSFIELD Yeah, the ground.

MIKEY No! Well yeah, it does. The deer does. But it hits a nerve. That sound. Like a monster deep down in the woods, ya know? Terrible. Terrible.

MANSFIELD Jesus.

Long pause.

MIKEY What a fucken mess, eh? *(beat.)* Ya see, Dev won't accept he done him in for twenty-seven poun'. He'll find somethin' here if it kills him.

MANSFIELD Yeah. He's proud.

MIKEY This is it. This is it.

Long pause.

Your Ma – did she – did she – what he said – ya know…
*(***MANSFIELD** *nods)*

MANSFIELD Aye. *(beat)* First time, she cut this way. *(indicates upwards along his arms)* That's the serious way. That isn't a cry for help. That's 'fuck you for finding me'. Then she drove her car into the river, and some Turkish sailor dragged her out. He'd just set foot in Ireland, imagine that? On the docks, and there she is, this woman in the river. Said he thought she looked like a mermaid down there. Said she was smiling. Was beautiful, like. Had all this seaweed shit in her hair. *(beat)* And then – in the place – in the place – she tied the laces round some hook on a bathroom door. They forgot about the shoes, ya see. It happens that way, sometimes, in those places. Sometimes they just forget about the shoes.

Long pause.

MIKEY There's a dog in the next room.

MANSFIELD What?

MIKEY A dog. In the next room.

MANSFIELD I heard ya. It just sounds so… a dog?

MIKEY Yeah. A little Jack Russell cowerin' under the bed. Just cowerin'. No bark nor nothin'. Saw him when me and Joe came up that first time. Nice dog. Scared shitless. Has a red collar and a little, ya know, tag. Just shakin' and cowerin' under the bed. Not a peep out of him. But I'd say when we go he'll go fucken mental. I tell ya one thing, I'm going to leave that door open and he'll get in and bark his fucken head off. One way or another – we'll go down for this, Terry. There is no way round that fucking fact.

Sound of the toilet flushing. The bulb flickers. **MIKEY** *and* **MANSFIELD** *watch.* **PRENTICE** *moves his head up from the floor and watches. This lasts for many seconds.*

The light goes out; a tinny pop sound. The room is now in full-dark.

FUCK!!

The sound of **PRENTICE** *breathing. Three or four raspy breaths.*

Blackout.

Scene Eight

MIKEY *crawls along floor, finds the upturned lamp switches it on (40 Watt).*

MANSFIELD We have to do something.

MIKEY What's fucken keeping them?

MANSFIELD *takes up a pillowcase, sees something inside, something very small, examines it, puts it in his pocket, is distracted a little - but carries on, uses the pillowcase to wipe blood from* **PRENTICE**. *Fixes the armchair and lifts* **PRENTICE** *to his feet and into the chair. Looks around for somewhere to sit so he can nurse and clean him, see what he's doing. He goes to a gas cylinder, lifts it a little but it is so heavy he drags it towards* **PRENTICE**, *sits down on it, wipes him further, tries to make him more comfortable.*

MANSFIELD Can you move your jaw? Try. (**PRENTICE** *tries to, nods that it's OK)*

He'll need a hospital.

MIKEY What he needs is a wet towel.

MIKEY *soaks another pillowcase in the remaining water, places it across* **PRENTICE**'s *head. He splashes some water onto his face and into his mouth.*

MANSFIELD He needs a hospital.

PRENTICE *coughs a little.*

MIKEY You wanna call them? Explain this? Go ahead.

PRENTICE No. Not necessary. *(clears his throat, works his jaw)* No. Just. A few cuts. Stomach. Leg, a bit. No more, though. End it now, eh?

MIKEY We want ta, Prentice. Just got outta hand. That's all.

PRENTICE Ah. Yer young. Think there's nothin' for yez. Only seems that way. *(beat)* Jonah Devlin's boy – nothin' like the mother I tell yez that. He's unreasonable. Somethin' – somethin' cold in him. He's got cold eyes. Like a seagull. Yez should get away from him. I see somethin' in him. Somethin' I shouldn't. *(coughs, clears his throat)*

MIKEY His da's a bad egg, Prentice.

PRENTICE He's not so bad, his da. I know him. Average bad maybe. Though it doesn't always follow the son is like the father, ya know. *(pause. Catches his breath)* Read somethin' one time. Shakespeare. *(slight beat)* 'Beneath the nettle the strawberry grows'.** Somethin' like that.

MIKEY What's it mean?

PRENTICE Means it doesn't always follow the son is like the father. Someone good *can* come from someone bad.

MANSFIELD Wish I could believe that.

MIKEY Not true with Dev. Total nettle he is. Through and through. Same as his da. No doubt about it.

PRENTICE Well then, the question is – what are the rest a yez? Strawberry – or nettle?

MIKEY Nettle.

PRENTICE You sure? Don't seem so bad to me.

MIKEY Ya don't know me. Ya don't know my da.

PRENTICE And you? How about you?

Beat.

** Correct quote:
The strawberry grows underneath the nettle,
And wholesome berries thrive and ripen best
Neighbored by fruit of baser quality.
Bishop of Ely, Henry V, act 1, sc. 1, l. 60–2.

MANSFIELD Same as my oul fella. Total nettle. Same as Jonah. No change.

PRENTICE Well, I think anyone be the nickname a Tolstoy would have to be more strawberry than nettle. And you're not anything like your father, far as I can see.

MANSFIELD Well, ya don't know me.

PRENTICE All nettle here then. No strawberries at all. I'm fucked so.

Long pause.

Now look. My dog. Don't…

MIKEY No, you look! We are the bad children, Prentice. Ya only read about us before. Well, we are 'em, ya understand? So shut up about your dog. I seen him. He'll be OK. I promise. So just shut up about him. *(long pause)* Why'd you come back here, huh? To this town and its bars, eh? It didn't need another bar. That wasn't very imaginative of ya, was it? A bar on a street of bars? I see them on this street, like a row of bog-holes all lined up. Little pits wall-to-wall with men like us in twenty years. The Congo! Maybe you shoulda stayed out there, huh? Bet you wish you had now. Some wide muddy river, some mud-hut somewhere. Better than this shithole.

PRENTICE Gimme a hard man's cigarette, will ya?

MIKEY *lights him up.*

I was there a while. Five years. Saw plenty of mud-huts. Stayed on even after they killed Lumumba.

MIKEY What he say?

MANSFIELD Lumumba. *(**MANSFIELD** points to the **PATRICE LUMUMBA** picture on the wall.)* Kinda like the Fidel Castro *(sees that **MIKEY** doesn't know this name either)* …

the Gerry Adams of the Congo. They assassinated him after two months runnin' the place.

PRENTICE That's right, yeah. Leopoldville I was in. The capital. Capital of hell. Never saw a more corrupt town in all my life. Where anybody did business with anybody, ya might say. Some say even Hitler's men were sold diamonds there by the Allies during the War. And well I'd believe it. A shithole ever I saw one. Rotten to the core. Yet it was – it is – so rich. You fellas – in here lookin' for somethin' I'm tellin' ya I don't have – that box is it – whatever's in that, that's it. But the Congo? Africa – the Katanga copper belt – so thick in the ground it was with copper nothin' would grow there. Nothing would grow! I used ta laugh at the irony of that. *(as he recalls that laughter and goes to laugh, he moans – his body is badly bruised. Sighs. Pause)* They hacked up his body, ya know. Dissolved the flesh in acid. And he *(points to picture of Lumumba)* was a remarkable man. They had a real chance with him. But hell had been there so long – we had been there so long – they knew nothin' else. A cesspit, a darkness, a pit of greed and consumption. You name the fiend, it lived there. Could see it in people's eyes. The lack of sleep from lyin' awake at night thinkin' up all the possibilities those diamonds and gold could offer. Well, a little dream of here is what kept me goin'. And not just buyin' a place like this. It was the sea. The smell of salt. The heather on the bogs up there. *(laughs, looks at his own battered body, coughs)* But the climates of places are different, that's all. Everywhere is Leopoldville, ya know? Everywhere. In Leopoldville I used to think there was a flaw in the design, the way people go on. But now, I just think it *is* the design. *(beat)* Kinshasa they call it now.

DEVLIN *has entered during* **PRENTICE**'s *speech*.

DEVLIN Well, would ya look at this. Fucken cosy corner. We should light a fire. Tell ghost stories. What about that, Prentice? Got some ghosty stories you can tell us, huh? You asked him where he put the money, Terry? No. Didn't think so. What about you, Mikey?

NO ANSWER.

All right. Joe! Gascy! Get in. Get in here now…

The sound of drums coming closer and closer. Once again, it is the rhythm of the intro of Joy Division's 'Atrocity Exhibition'.

JOE *and* **GASCOIGNE** *enter the room playing the drums. They are semi-naked, no trousers or shoes,* **GASCOIGNE** *is wrapped in a rug,* **JOE** *in the leopard-skin from the room next door. They have chalk stripes on their faces and forehead. The overall effect is mock-African tribal costume.* **GASCOIGNE** *wears a fez, is drinking from a bottle of vodka, and holds a spear, he is also wearing a red dog collar with a tag.* **DEVLIN** *grabs the vodka off* **GASCOIGNE***, takes a swig, offers the bottle to* **MANSFIELD***, who declines.* **DEVLIN** *thrusts it on to* **JOE***, who drinks it down,* **MIKEY** *grabs the vodka off* **JOE***, chucks it to one side.*

PRENTICE *(sits up and looks at the dog collar, lets out a long sob)* Sailor! Sailor! Oh, God what have yez done!

JOE *and* **GASCOIGNE** *prance around the room idiotically, banging the drums, the gear slipping off them, chanting:*

This is the way, step inside. This is the way, step inside. Fee- fi – fo – fum – I smell the blood of a publican.

GASCOIGNE I liked lickle doggy, Joe. I feel sorry about lickle doggy. I do.

JOE Just think about the money and you'll be all right, Gascy.

JOE AND GASCOIGNE This is the way, step inside. This is the way, step inside. Fi-fi-fo-fum I smell the blood of a publican.

MIKEY *(to* **JOE***)* You fucking idiot! You put him up ta this, Dev. He'd not think of this. No, this is more up your street. Like the bananas. Like all that weird fucking shit you do.

DEVLIN Give it an oul thump, Gascy. That's it. Oh, you're looking powerful fellas. Thumpety-thump, thumpety-thump.

JOE *and* **GASCOIGNE** *proceed to dress* **PRENTICE** *up in the skin and fez, as if he were an African 'King' on his throne, the spear his sceptre.*

JOE Tell ya one thing money-bags. There's one little doggy won't be lickin' your face. Won't be alertin' passers-by neither when we're gone. Which is what ya probably wanted, I'd say. So I had to do it, see. We'll need time to get outta here, won't we, Dev? Can't be given away early by no scabby dog.

JOE *and* **GASCOIGNE** *dance round him drumming in a frenzied way. Chants of FI-FI-FO-FUM etc.*

MANSFIELD Leave him alone. Leave him! (**JOE** *pushes* **MANSFIELD** *to one side.*)

MIKEY That's it. I'm off. I'm done. You're on your own, Joe. Always were a fucken liability to me.

MIKEY *goes to leave and is stopped by* **DEVLIN** *at the door.*

DEVLIN Now where d'you think you're goin'?

MIKEY Out of this mad house. Do what ya like with him. Do. What. You. Like. As of this moment he's no brother a mine. Terry, come on. This'll not get better.

How can it? Don't wait for the fucken worst. Don't wait for the fucken worst.

DEVLIN Alls he has do is tell us where he –

MIKEY Shut up! Shut up! Shut! Up! You don't know him! He's seen the whole world and what you seen? Nothin'! Just like me. What I want with his money? I don't care! All I want is ta get out!

DEVLIN You are a part of it. You stayed. You watched it happen.

MIKEY I'm only here because little drummer-boy there happens to be my kid brother!

DEVLIN Don't blame it on Joe, you fucken coward.

MANSFIELD So what is all a this, Dev? Is it for the money? Here. Here. *(throws some of his own money at him)* Want more? I'll write you a fucking cheque.

JOE Gone back to his old ways. Throwin' money at a problem. Ya must be the problem so, Dev.

DEVLIN Seems that way, Joe.

MANSFIELD Prentice! Listen you old fool! I'm sorry about your dog. But, come on, this has gotta end. Come on! Have ya money ya haven't told us about? Please, for the love of god! Please!

PRENTICE *begins to sing (still crying over the dog, as if to swallow the pain, distract himself)*

IN THE FEMALE PRISON
THERE ARE SEVENTY WOMEN
I WISH IT WAS WITH THEM THAT I DID DWELL
AND THAT AULD TRIANGLE
WENT JINGLE JANGLE
ALONG THE BANKS OF THE ROYAL...

DEVLIN *kicks* **PRENTICE**'s *chair over, so that* **PRENTICE**'s *legs are in the air, the back of the chair on the floor.* **MANSFIELD** *sighs in disgust. No more singing.*

DEVLIN Ya see 'please' is just a formality, Terry. A mask. Or part of a code, ya might say. A code us nice people use ta get through the day without killin' each other. But look around ya: no code now, have we boys? Well, we do, but it's the simplest code of them all. It's the I'm-the-fucking-King-now-code, and alls youse have to do is the next simplest code of them all, the do-what-I-fucking-say-if-ya-want-a-life-worth-living code.

JOE places the fez from PRENTICE's head onto DEVLIN's. JOE and GASCOIGNE circle DEVLIN, drumming. DEVLIN steps up onto a barrel/cylinder. PRENTICE's breathing becoming heavier, raspier. He is coughing a lot now, and groans from the floor.

MANSFIELD Stop! Stop drumming!

JOE AND GASCOIGNE Dev's the King, Dev's the King, Dev's the King of the Congo. Dev's the King, Dev's the King, Dev's the King of the Congo.

DEVLIN acts up, preening, becomes all 'Kingly'.

JOE and GASCOIGNE alternate the two chants: 'This is the way, step inside' etc, with 'Dev's the King, Dev's the King' etc.

MANSFIELD *(above the chant)* Said you'd watch over me! Said the same to him too! But he doesn't mean it, Gascy! He's not your angel, he's not. They're just words. Words that spill from his mouth like old breath. STOP DRUMMING. STOP IT. STOP IT!!!

The drumming and DEVLIN's preening continue.

DEVLIN God is young! God. Is. Young!

MANSFIELD picks up the canister of gas. He is trying to make an impact, to get through to PRENTICE amid all the noise and chaos.

MANSFIELD Endgame! Endgame! Tell us now Prentice, and tell us quick. For Christ's sake! Hurry!

PRENTICE Ya know what they did, young fella? Bundled Lumumba into the back of a car at night during a tropical rainstorm. Some say it was his own friends that done it. That night – is as clear to me as this moment: the rain on my window, falling in hard drops like diamonds. What we did out there! Oh, don't ya get it, kid? It's my time! The devil is in the room. G'wan then! Do it. End it all. End it <u>please</u>. *(in a sing-songey, chant-like voice)* Kill, kill, kill. I left my soul in Leopoldville. *(laughs)* Hey Dev, I'm a poet and I didn't know it.

MANSFIELD's *hands and arms are trembling while holding the canister, his adrenalin is running out. Moves closer. Hangs it over* **PRENTICE**. **PRENTICE** *starts to sing:*

AND THAT AULD TRIANGLE
WENT JINGLE JANGLE
ALONG THE BANKS OF THE ROYAL CANAL.

JOE *and* **GASCOIGNE**'s *chant continues. Together this and* **PRENTICE**'s *song create a violent discordance. For instance: 'This is the way step inside'/ 'Along the banks of the Royal Canal'.*

MANSFIELD *steps back, brings down the canister and collapses in a heap.* **MIKEY** *rushes towards* **JOE**, *knocks his costume off, wipes chalk off his face, drags him to the door, kicking and screaming.*

JOE We were just messin', Mikey! We were! Listen, the dog... the dog...

MIKEY Terry! Terry! Move it. Come on, man.

MANSFIELD *gets up rushes to doorway and stops by* **DEVLIN**. **MIKEY** *still clinging to* **JOE** *by the door.*

MIKEY Come on, Terry. Terry, lets go! *(*MANSFIELD *hesitates)*

DEVLIN Don't…

MANSFIELD What you say?

DEVLIN … leave. Don't leave.

MANSFIELD Don't leave *what?*

DEVLIN *(nervously)* Don't go.

MANSFIELD Don't go *what?*

Pause.

(shouts) I can't hear you, Dev!

DEVLIN *(shouts)* Don't. Leave. Terry. (**DEVLIN** *goes slowly towards* **MANSFIELD**, *goes to touch his shoulder or hair, stops short behind him.*) Please. (**DEVLIN** *turns his face away, his head bowed*)

JOE God, Dev! Dev? Whatya doin', huh? God!

Then **GASCOIGNE** *rushes in, picks up the canister. He is much stronger than* **MANSFIELD**, *and it is easy for him to lift it. He drops the canister on* **PRENTICE***'s head. (which we don't see as the front of the chair should obscure the fall of the cylinder)*

Silence.

GASCOIGNE *backs off and screams.* **JOE** *rushes in, puts his hand over* **GASCOIGNE***'s mouth.*

DEVLIN Oh, oh you… you… ya shouldn't have done that Gascy.

Silence.

MIKEY *goes over to* **PRENTICE**. *Tries to look under canister, gets up, turns his head away as if to puke.*

Oh, not just Prentice that's dead now, is it boys? Thanks to that, to that stupid rich cunt we're all fucked.

JOE Mikey! Listen... the dog... the dog...

MIKEY Shut up about it, Joe!

MANSFIELD Oh, Gascy! I wasn't going to drop it. I, I only wanted to scare him!

Long pause.

Ah, man. There's no air in here. And – and look at the cut of the place. It was all the noise! Those drums! How could he think straight, huh? How could I?

GASCOIGNE He won't take the piss outta the bad children now, Dev, will he? That'll teach him, won't it Dev. That'll teach him. *(he sobs)*

DEVLIN Why'd ya go near a thing like that at all for Terry, huh?

MANSFIELD I wasn't going ta drop it was I?!

DEVLIN Your lily-white hands are not so clean though, are they? All this. For the money you said was here.

MANSFIELD I never said there was money!

DEVLIN You never said there wasn't!

JOE *(who has been hovering over* **PRENTICE***)* There's stuff, bits of head – everyplace. All over the floor. Ah God.

GASCOIGNE *(goes to* **PRENTICE***, closer than the others have done, touches him gently)* All his dreams, Joe. Everythin' he seen in the whole world. He won't dream no more now. He won't miss the lickle doggy. He won't anything.

Long pause.

JOE Tolstoy's father's a solicitor! He's gonna be fine! Not us though.

DEVLIN Yeah. That's how it will go, Joe. Isn't that just somethin'? *(pause)* Come on. Lets get outta here.

Outta this stinkhole. *(to* **MANSFIELD***, with his steely toughness resumed)* Hey. Hey you. Terry. *(***MANSFIELD** *stands defiantly, does not look at* **DEVLIN***)*

Beat.

Never mind. *(***DEVLIN** *exits)*

JOE *goes to* **MIKEY**.

JOE It was just meant to have been a laugh!

MIKEY Who's laughin'? Get dressed. Two a yez. Ya look ridiculous. Get Gascy home. Who has the knife?

JOE I do.

MIKEY Hide it in a side of turf up there in the bogs. Go up straight after ya leave him home, ya hear?

JOE Aye. Aye. I'm sorry, Mikey… *(he sobs)*… I shouldn't a…

MIKEY Won't be there for ya all yer days, Joe. Can't. If we get sent down you'll be on yer own. Alone in some fucken cell, ya understand?

JOE *leads* **GASCOIGNE** *out.* **MIKEY** *and* **MANSFIELD** *are alone.*

Silence.

MIKEY Come on. We need to get out.

MANSFIELD Yeah. Give me a minute will ya? Just one minute. Here. That's all.

He mutters:

Prentice, Prentice, Prentice, Prentice, Prentice.

MIKEY Oh the weight of it. The weight of that thing on a man's skull. Like a bomb.

MIKEY *turns to leave.* **MANSFIELD** *stops him.* **MANSFIELD** *opens up his hand and holds out a small stone, the size of a quail's egg.*

What is it?

MANSFIELD Found it in the pillow. They look like this. Diamonds. When they come out of the earth. I read about it. All pink and brown and uncut. And cold to the touch. Here. You can see when you rub. Some kind of light trying to get out.

MIKEY You shoulda said somethin'. Before. You shoulda said.

MANSFIELD I got confused. Didn't know what to do. Give it to Devlin? I hated him today. I didn't before, Mikey. No, I... but I am so fucking confused now. Oh, the pressure in my head.

MIKEY *(shouts):* Yeah? Tell that to him!

Pause.

MANSFIELD *(holding out the stone):* Look at it. What do I do with this, huh? Leave it here? I don't want it. Maybe I could put it back where... where Prentice had... *(looks to the bed, to* **PRENTICE** *on the floor beside it)* Oh, Christ! He was a good man, Mikey. All he wanted was his little bar. What did we do here in the name of God?

Long pause.

Here. You take it.

MIKEY What use is that to me? Probably not real anyways. He would have said.

MANSFIELD Take it! Come on. You could sell it. *(***MIKEY** *shakes his head)* What about the girl? The house with the fuchsia, and the turf outside? Of all of us, Mikey – you could have that happy life. Take the stone! *(***MIKEY**

shakes his head again.) What did you do here? Nothing. Nothing that I could see.

MIKEY *doesn't take the stone.*

MIKEY Come on. We need to go. *(he exits)*

MANSFIELD *walks over to the window, opens the curtains. Daylight fills the room, exposing the horror within in the most pedestrian way.* **MANSFIELD** *stares for several seconds at this newly illuminated scene, as a dog begins to bark in the next room.*

Fade lights.

The End

Property List

Cemetery – Gascoigne is tied to an iron Celtic cross (p1)
Box of bananas, skins scattered everywhere, a banana mess on Gascoigne's clothes (p1)
Two half-peeled bananas (p1)
Cigarettes / smoking (p1)
Bottle of whiskey (p1)
Watch (p1)
Vault wall (p2)
Cigarettes (p4)
Used tissue (p4)
Coat (p5)
Inside of a bar (p8)
Sign – 'The Congo' in large black letters - background image of mountains with an image of a drum in the foreground (p8)
Breast-high bar with a brass rail (p8)
Silver faux antique cash register (p8)
Assortment of drinks at the back (p8)
Red leather seats (p8)
Red velvet topped bar stools (p8)
Tables (p8)
A faded wooden floor (p8)
A number of black and white photos of a man in exotic places getting off planes and ships etc. (p8)
Two small drums (p8)
A dartboard and blackboard – with a little ledge, which holds pieces of chalk and a case of darts (p8)
Half curtains (p9)
Crisp packets hanging up behind the bar (p9)
Couple of beers (p9)
Knife (p11)
Till (p12)
A few notes (p12)
Coke on tap (p13)

Ice (p14)
Darts and dartboard (p17)
Two pint glasses (p18)
Cokes and salt and vinegar crisps (p18)
Bolts on the door (p20)
Key in the door (p20)
Glass of water (p28)
Smashes bottles at the back of the bar (p28)
Money (p31)
Joe taking pictures off the wall and dropping them (p32)
Cigarette (p36)
Three darts (p40)
Blood and white feathers on their hands (p43)
Large map of Africa in the shape of Patrick Lumumba's head (p46)
A double bed (p46)
Radio on the small bedside (p46)
Built-in wardrobe (p46)
Sideboard with upturned photos (p46)
Upturned bedside lamp (p46)
Gas cylinders (p46)
Barrel (p46)
Busted pillows, feathers (p46)
Cuts up a pillow with a knife, throws some feathers (p47)
Water (p51)
Floorboards by the window have been pulled up (p53)
Box (p53)
Key (p53)
Note (p53)
Two cigarettes (p53)
Mikey soaks another pillowcase in the remaining water, places it across Prentice's head (p60)

Picture of Lumumba (p63)
Bottle of vodka (p64)
Money (p66)
Fez hat (p67)

Costume:

Prentice Black – suit, white shirt and braces (p24)

Devlin and Joe – blood and white feathers all over their hands (p43)

Gascoigne – new jacket – checked lining (p44)

Prentice Black – blood on his face, chest and legs. Feathers stuck to him (p46)

Joe and Gascoigne – they are semi-naked. No trousers or shoes. Gascoigne is wrapped in a rug. Joe in the leopard-skin from the room next door. They have chalk stripes on their faces and forehead. The overall effect is mock-African tribal costume. Gascoigne wears a fez, he is drinking from a bottle of vodka, and holds a spear. He is also wearing a red dog collar with a tag (p64)

Lighting

Moonlit (p1)

Both are isolated in their own pools of light (p1)

Fade lights (p7)

The light picks out no detail of his face or figure, so that his momentary stance in the doorway is shadowy and ominous (p8)

Blackout (p16)

Blackout (p23)

Blackout (p39)

Blackout (p45)

Bare central bulb (p46)

Darkness (p46)

Joe puts on the light (60 Watt) (p46)

Blackout (p52)

Bulb flickers (p58)

The light goes out (p59)

Blackout (p59)

The room is now in full-dark (p59)

Mikey…finds the upturned lamp switches it on (40 Watt) (p60)

Mansfield….opens the curtains. Daylight exposes the carnage in the room (p72)

Fade lights (p72)

Sound Effects

Door opening slowly (p8)

The bell of the bar rings out (p8)

Sounds of the other two stamping around the room upstairs (p10)

Joe and Mikey can be heard screaming and roaring (p11)

Commotion outside the door – sound of Prentice Black (p22)

Screams heard from upstairs. Smashed glasses, a rumble, Devlin's voice. Angry and fast. Then Joe's manic laughter, followed by three loud smacks and more screams (p40)

Silence (p40)

Knock on the door (p43)

Another knock (p43)

Another knock (p43)

Sound of the toilet flushing (p58)

A tinny pop sound (p59)

Sound of drums coming closer and closer (p64)

A dog barks in the next room (p72)

www.ingramcontent.com/pod-product-compliance
Ingram Content Group UK Ltd.
Pitfield, Milton Keynes, MK11 3LW, UK
UKHW021835210426
5322IPUK00021B/300